With O'Leary in the Grave

Kevin FitzGerald

*Romantic Ireland's dead and gone,
It's with O'Leary in the grave.*

W. B. YEATS
'September 1913'

Michael Russell

© Kevin FitzGerald 1986

First published in Great Britain 1986
by Michael Russell (Publishing) Ltd.,
The Chantry, Wilton, Salisbury, Wiltshire

Typeset by the Bournemouth Acorn Press Ltd
Printed and bound in Great Britain
by Biddles Ltd., Guildford and King's Lynn

For Prudence

Contents

Author's Note

This book would never have been published without the help of my friend Philip Mason. I lost my sight just as the typescript of the first draft reached me. Philip took on the job of editing it and looking after the business details and I cannot let it appear without recording my thanks for this demonstration of friendship.

K.F.

Introduction

When Kevin FitzGerald began to write *With O'Leary in the Grave* his sight was already failing. By the time he had finished he was totally blind and the problems of blindness at over eighty were such that it was quite impossible for him to undertake the revision he knew it needed. I asked if I might see it; I was soon convinced that it ought to be shared with a wider public and I asked if I might do the revision. I have ironed out a few creases but tried to keep the tone of his voice.

I am prejudiced about this book because I have enjoyed Kevin's conversation so much for so long. But I have tried to put myself in the place of a stranger. He, I think, should come to it expecting the pleasure of conversation with an original mind about varied experiences. It is essentially conversation; Kevin writes very much as he talks. It is a book about a most unusual father and an unusual son, one that displays, enormously magnified, the tensions between every father and son. There have been many strange fathers in fiction and autobiography but surely none stranger than Kevin's; he is rich comedy to read about and the story races whenever he is holding forth. But he must have been almost unbearable in the flesh and it is astonishing that Kevin put up with him so long. Can he be true? Can any father in literature be true? Can you believe that Sir George Sitwell was really the man portrayed by Sir Osbert? Can Philip Gosse have been quite as Edmund Gosse describes him in *Father and Son*? But in Kevin's case there is good supporting evidence. 'My mother' is a character of rare beauty, drawn with great economy, and it is quite clear that, though she adored him and though *she* could manage him, she perceived how impossible her husband was for anyone else to deal with.

The family alone would be enough, but this is a rich book and I shall not forget the Dean of Cashel and his black bottle, nor the dreadful Professor Drummond – nor Kevin standing before him in disgrace in his beautiful apron, lovingly embroidered by Miss

Ireland because 'he must look nice for the Professor' – nor Mike McTigue of Tubberadora and his cow. We go back to a vanished Ireland, a land of outside cars and horse shows, of ass-carts and all-night dances, of bitter quarrels and tearful reconciliations.

Above all, there is the ploughing with horses. That first day's ploughing at Synone is a lyrical account of a day of pure happiness – something rare in literature, like the wolf-hunt in *War and Peace*. But the intensity of feeling is backed by accurate technical detail carefully observed, about the land-horse and the furrow-horse, about swingletrees and the mould board. That is a recipe for good writing. And there is the heroic spell on the prairie in Canada, with Mr Innes, another unforgettable figure sketched with a few strokes. There is the brief spell as a lorry-driver in Cockney London, where his mates called Kevin 'Duke', perhaps in recognition of the tones of the Oratory School – perhaps in slightly mocking tribute to simplicity and generosity of character. Yes, it is a rich book.

But an autobiography must in the end be about one person. This is a very human person, gloriously inconsistent, shot through by ambivalence, loving and admiring his father though constantly infuriated and frustrated, just as mixed in his love of Ireland and admiration for England, in his deep Catholicism and impatience with the Church. He once told me of a Dublin friend who decided during Hitler's War to apply for a commission in the Irish Guards. Once commissioned, he was trained in parachute-jumping. 'Five thousand pounds they spent training me!' he said. 'Five thousand pounds, Kevin my boy! And when they had me trained, they put me in an aeroplane and dropped me over a place they called Arnhem. As I came to the ground, five bullets went slap into my belly. And I rolled over on the ground and said to myself: "Thank God the so-and-sos will never get a penny piece worth of value out of me!"' 'Now, what', Kevin ended triumphantly, 'can you do with people like us?'

Any account of a man's life by himself must be unfinished. As he writes the last word, no man knows what still awaits him. And this book ends before Kevin is thirty. It was written with the clear intention of writing more – and indeed there already is some more. But for the moment, the book must stand on its own, and the reader is bound to ask some questions about a man for whom by the end he is likely to feel an affection. And to two of his questions it seems to me that he ought to have an answer.

Kevin has given me the answers. He came back from Canada penniless but triumphant. He had not starved on the prairie; he had made good; he had proved his father wrong. Mr Innes had advised him to go back because there was a nice, fat, easy living waiting for him in the Old Country. So there would have been if his father had been anyone else. But after eighteen months at Synone, Kevin said to his mother: 'I am becoming a man on a horse riding about the place doing nothing. I am beginning to think I must get away from here.' 'To my consternation, she said: "Yes, dear, you must. There will never be anything here for you."' She was right; she was as clear-eyed as ever. He left Synone and was soon appointed to a post with I.C.I., then only a year old. He was with I.C.I. for the rest of his life, for one long spell as Agricultural Manager for the South-East of England, later as General Manager in Ireland, and finally as Head of Agricultural Publicity for I.C.I. and Plant Protection. With the left hand, as it were, he wrote a number of thrillers that sold well, did a good deal of broadcasting and became a mountaineer.

That explains the note of doom about Synone. His father quite forgot that he had bought it for Kevin and it went to his elder brother. There is another recurrent note of doom, which becomes very loud in the story of Mike O'Ryan, the carpenter at Mr Willington's place, St Kierans. Once a quarter Mike would leave his work for a week for a terrible bout of drinking. Drink became a problem for Kevin too; he too had his occasional bouts and he decided that he must give up alcohol entirely. He had not had a drink for four years when he first heard of Alcoholics Anonymous and began to help others who wanted to stop drinking but found it hard.

That is all about the future that anyone needs to know. But is the book tragedy or comedy? *O'Leary* makes me laugh in every chapter yet ends with the word 'Alas!'. Ought we to cry at the end for the waste and frustration? We are bound, I think, to wish that Kevin had been allowed to be the master of Synone, riding about the fields, taking a turn now and then for Mick Barratt behind the plough, winning prizes at shows with Aberdeen Angus bulls and Large White sows. And yet – he would not have become a mountaineer; many friends would never have met him. I cannot regret it altogether. Still less can I feel regret that he did not start farming by himself on a quarter-section in Canada.

My own feeling about *With O'Leary in the Grave* is very like Dr Johnson's about London. If you do not find things to like in this book, you must be tired of life.

PHILIP MASON

One

My father was usually a rich man. But there were times when he was that strange phenomenon, a rich man without a penny. Then there would be talk about emigration, ruin, country cottages and, above all, the cutting down of other people's wasteful expenditure.

I was the last of his children and I must have arrived in one of the better periods. My first memory is of standing on the lawn at the back of a big house and knowing that I lived there. I was watching my father shoot arrows right over the house. He had made the bow for me, but I was too young and weak to use it. It seemed a wonderful thing to do; it now seems highly dangerous. The house must have been Grove Lodge in Stamford Hill, a big stone house with a half-moon carriage drive, two sets of high double entrance gates, and an enclosing wall. There was a door let into this wall which was operated by a mysterious arrangement of wires in the kitchen. The visitor rang a bell set high above the door, someone in the house pulled a handle, there was a loud click and the door flew open. I lived in this house until I was seven and a half and I was never tall enough to ring the bell if I got accidentally shut out into Grove Lane. On those rare occasions I was at the mercy of kindly passers-by.

I played in the garden of this house all day long, sometimes with my sister Carrie, sometimes with Vincent, our gardener, who later became what was then known as an 'engineer' and drove the UNIC car my father bought, in, I suppose, 1905. Vincent took a poor view of my Holland overalls which he seemed to think, in discussions with Bella, my nurse, or with Mary, or Mrs Tomasi, might have a strange effect on my sexual development. I daresay they did.

When I was five my eldest brother Will became twenty-one and there was a tremendous all-night party at Grove Lodge. For days I followed Vincent about as he hung huge Japanese lanterns from every tree and put up rows and rows of coloured glass

pots, each of which held a night-light. Each night-light had 'Price. Six hours' printed on it. I remember that because I was allowed to drop them into the little pots.

There was a platform built on the lawn and a piano was wheeled out to it on the day. It seemed to me that hundreds of people came, and that they all brought my brother trouser presses which were put on the billiard table my father had given him. I didn't know my eldest brother then; he was working in the north of England, training to enter my father's business. My Uncle Tom, who had a very deep bass voice, sang a song about 'Down in the Dust' and my brother Tom, who was going to be a priest, and was always called Tommy All Souls because he was born on November 2nd, sang a song called 'The Other Department If You Please'. No one took the slightest notice of me all through the party.

My father's father – I never thought of him as my grandfather – was in the Royal Navy. He had fought in the Crimean War and had been in Captain Peel's famous landing party in the redoubt at Sebastopol. I only saw him once, sitting with my grandmother Honora. I had no difficulty in thinking about *her* as my grandmother and she still frightened me a little when I was quite grown up. When my father's father retired they put him in charge of a coast-guard centre at Minehead. My father was born in Tenby in South Wales, while my grandmother was trying to get over to Ireland to have him born on that sacred soil.

All my father's brothers were born in England and all of them died young except Uncle Patrick. They all seem to have 'liked a drink' because my grandmother never let my father's father have one. I remember that clearly, and that my father used to give him secret glasses of whisky. My father himself never drank anything. I expect if he had told us why, none of us would have begun drinking either. As it was we all lived to regret our first drink.

I must have been over thirty when I heard why my father was a total abstainer. He had heard a woman say, just after his twenty-first birthday: 'Look at that huge red-bearded Irishman, drunk the way they always are.' He had his next drink when he was seventy-five. I was with him and saw him have it. We were lunching in his club and he suddenly called the wine waiter and said: 'Bring me a pint of Tolley, and put it in a pint glass; I want to see it.' When it came he held it up to the light and said to me 'Look at that, my son. Shining like a ruby in a rajah's turban.' Then he drank it in one long swallow and told me about the woman saying he was drunk.

All my father's early life remained a secret. He never even told my mother about it. Over the years we put bits of it together. They were poor in Minehead, and he ran away from home when he was a little boy. He used to say that when he was young the moon was made of solid gold, 'and you reached up a hand, my son, and broke pieces off it'. Once he said to me: 'I always meant to make £100,000 before I was forty, but I actually made a quarter of a million.' Money wasn't money to my father, but a set of counters which allowed him to sit in at games which interested him. One thing he enjoyed doing, and I enjoyed seeing when I was small, was throwing a handful of sovereigns into my mother's apron. She would hold it out and he would throw the sovereigns across the room. 'That was what we used to do when I was first married,' she said.

My father was already engaged to be married when he first saw my mother. It must have been at a party, because he pulled a cracker with her and a ring fell out of it. My mother's father had been a sea captain, in the Merchant Service, trading into the Baltic, Dutch and German North Sea ports, but he was already dead when my father began calling night after night at their little house. There they lived, the three sisters and my Uncle Tom, all very happy, snug and poor. Mother told me that there came at last the dreadful night of her birthday and her mother's appalling words: 'He has broken off his engagement to that other woman and I think he means to take advantage of you. If he does not give you a ring for your birthday, I shall think nothing of him, and you must never see him again.' 'Well, of course, dear,' my mother said when she told me the story, 'I was in love with your father by then, and I knew that he wasn't the man to be carrying rings about for me, and I dreaded his arrival all day; almost hoped he wouldn't come at all. But he did, and we set off on the dreary walk we had taken most nights for two or three months. We lived in a poor part, dear,' my mother said, 'long empty streets with gas lamps. And it was raining, as it nearly always is on my birthday.' She was born in January, 1862. 'So at last he stopped under a lamp and took a little box out of his pocket and said, "I've bought you a present for your birthday, Cassie." My heart went to my boots, as they say, because it was the wrong sort of box. I stood under the lamp and opened it and I thought, when I saw what was there, that I wouldn't dare go home, and what was to become of me. Because all there was in the box was a painted oyster shell with the new Tower Bridge on it. I don't think I cried because I loved your father and it was his present, but I felt dreadful. Then he said: "There's something written on the back you ought to read." So I took out the shell, and there was this lovely diamond ring.' Mother held up her left hand. 'He took it out of the box and put it on my finger and said, "We're engaged to be married, Cassie" and then I did cry. After a bit I said: "How did you know what size ring to buy?" and he said: "I knew I was going to marry you when we pulled the cracker, and you remember we tried on the cracker ring for fun." And then, dear, he took the cracker ring out of his waist-coat pocket and showed it to me. He had kept it all that time.'

My father was like that all his life. Years later my sister Netta wanted one of the long gold chains which were popular with young women at the time. No one could ever get Netta on to paper but the effort will have to be made. She was certain my father would give her a chain because she had been letting him know what she wanted ever since October and now it was Christmas morning. My father solemnly handed Netta a pair of gloves, and she burst into tears and rushed out of the room. 'Come back and try them on; I may have to change them,' my father shouted, and the beautiful tearful figure returned. Of course the chain, a fine and splendid one, was hidden inside the left-hand glove. My father liked power and he liked to use it and be seen to use it.

Before that we had left Grove Lodge. I expect we were ruined again. I don't know where my father went, but Mother and Netta and Carrie and I were all taken to Turner's Hall near Harpenden, where the farmer who had married my mother's dead sister, 'Midge', conducted what he seemed to think was farming. He spent most of the time holding off his housekeeper, who wanted to marry him and apparently wooed him with semolina pudding. We had it every day, and my mother remembered it all the rest of her life and even on her death bed. It was a poor place altogether, the land poor and badly farmed. I can still hear the farting of the broken-winded horse which drove us into Harpenden, to meet a train where my father would step from a first-class carriage, looking superior in top hat and frock coat.

Then we moved to Hurlingham Court on the Thames at Putney, a very grand, very large, furnished flat. Then came another time of major crisis; my father was once again irretrievably ruined and was building a tiny cottage for my mother in the wilds of Hertfordshire, in a place called Radlett. Bella came with us to Hurlingham Court, but not Mary. Mrs Tomasi reappeared in my life, always weeping, her son being then in prison. I didn't of course know then, as I was to learn later, that my father had arrangements about criminals with nearly all the redemption societies. I was later to become accustomed to being met at stations by burglars, confidence tricksters, reformed drunkards, and other employees of my father's. If she had known it, Mrs Tomasi's son was already on velvet. For years, every time he came out, my father would be setting him up.

But there we were in Hurlingham Court, with me, a boy of seven and a half, watching the university crews practising for the Boat Race, but much preferring the squat little tugs, pulling strings of barges, going up river with coal on every tide. It was always thrilling to watch the funnels being pulled down for Putney Bridge. I remember the boat crews, Mrs Tomasi weeping into grates, the tugs and their funnels, and a great voice at the other end of a speaking tube in the kitchen. 'Good morning,' it would declaim, 'Ironside the grocer at your service.' Everything was delivered in those days, arriving at the flat in a tiny box lift which discharged through a hatch in the kitchen. I used to hear the whistle blow, and rush out to greet the lift and help Bella take off 'the things'. All that was in 1909.

One day we all went to St Pancras Station and, after about an hour, the little train arrived at Radlett. Here we were greeted by the station master, Mr Hodge. The Midland Railway of those days did an enormous coal trade and could afford to make much of its passengers. All of us, Mother, Carrie my eldest sister, Netta and I, piled into an old growler and drove up an unmade clay road to a house in a field. That was Desmond Cottage, my mother's 'tiny country cottage' as my father always called it. It had five bedrooms to begin with, and two sitting rooms. But things must have looked up almost at once because my first memories of Desmond Cottage are of perpetual builders adding bits here and there. My father soon added another two bedrooms, built over another large sitting room. That gave him a library, all fitted bookcases and rare books. No one seemed to think we were poor.

My mother was the gentlest creature but always got her way in the end. People were always sending for her so that they could die in her arms. She had a private religion of her own which never seemed – to a very religious little boy well under the influence of nuns – to have much to do with the Roman Catholic Church as expounded at the convent. It had less and less to do with it as time went on, but she always liked going to Mass and, better still, sitting by herself in a church. Her surviving sister was a nun and eventually became a headmistress and an assistant mother superior. That aunt I never really knew; she never understood my name, calling me Kelvin, and I had not seen her for twenty-five years when she died. Mother Sebastian she was called in religion, which was nothing to the names of the two women responsible for what learning my mother possessed. One was Mother Crown of Thorns,* the other Mother Five Wounds. No wonder I grew up a rather tepid Catholic.

I grew up in Radlett, but never took much part in its social life. Not that there was a great deal of social life. There were a few residential houses dotted about, several belonging to my father though it was a long time before we discovered that. The village shops consisted of a grocer's with a sub-post office in it; Mr Porter's that was. There was a Co-operative store; the rudest chemist in England; Mr Massey, who had a tobacco and newspaper shop and cut hair; and a baker. Two sisters kept a little sweet shop and sold ice cream cornets for a penny; it was a coin that went a long way in those days.

On Sundays we all went to Mass, held in a tiny bedroom in a little house in the Radlett 'Cross-path'. A priest came over from St Albans on a bicycle to say it, and after our first week always came back to Desmond Cottage for breakfast. Before he left St Albans he said Mass in the new Catholic church of St Antony of

*She must really have been Mother Ursula of the Crown of Thorns, or something of the kind.   P.M.

22

Padua, also in the Cross-path. It was a hideous building, constructed under the will of a man to whose memory a dreadful stained glass window was placed in the west wall. My father bought the land for the church with plenty of room for any extensions which might become necessary as the population grew. He also provided the altar and most of the furnishings.

Radlett grew. The commuter age was upon us and as time went on more and more people in Radlett seemed to be always running to catch trains. I was never good at catching trains and I never really fitted in to Radlett. I always felt a stranger there.

I can't remember much about my first school, the tiny school at the top of Shenley Hill, except that every day I had to pass a house with a white dog which hated me. Each time I approached the house I prayed that the dog would be inside and shut up. He never was. He was always out in the garden waiting for me. Like all other dogs in the world, this dog wouldn't hurt a fly, but that didn't stop him, the first time I passed when his garden gate was open, from rushing out and burying his teeth in my behind.

'It's not as if he'd really bitten you, dear,' my mother said, 'lots of pretty little teeth marks, but your skin is not even broken.' We were what Mother called 'new here' and what that means in England is that no fuss must be made. My mother was what she herself called a 'peace-at-any-price-er', and it seems to me now that she had the right idea. For many years I have watched our freedoms being steadily eroded, almost entirely as a result of Stands Taken, Tyrants Faced, Enemies Broken, Truth and Honour Upheld.

Of that part of my schooling nothing remains but a fixed devotion to Her present Majesty's former physiotherapist. I still see her now – tall, calm, beautiful, in a huge picture hat. I used to walk up Shenley Hill with her, my hand in hers, heaven in my heart. I was then eight and a half, and the serious theological misgivings of all Catholics were beginning to afflict my parents. Where, in neighbouring Hertfordshire, could I obtain an education based on the Faith and a Catholic upbringing? Nowhere, it seemed, and I must be condemned to be a child with a season ticket hung round his neck, and travel daily with my sister Carrie to a convent of German nuns, the Poor Handmaidens of Jesus Christ, in Hendon. This was St Joseph's and the Jesuits must be right, because everything I learned there, except the German language, remains with me. All the basic prayers, of course, and all the Legends as well. It is sad to have been an authority all one's life on St Philomena, only to find at sixty-five that she never existed and must be removed from the prayers of the Church. No matter, St Philomena has been a good friend.

Sister Emerentia, Sister Gertrude and Sister Paula had never even heard of Saints Kevin and Columba, with whose tiresome names my life has been burdened. It appeared that there were, or had been, German saints – a likely story! I learned at St Joseph's about the wickedness of a certain Herr Wagner and I acquired a hatred of gravy, from which I have never recovered, and an inability to go to bed without saying at least some of my night prayers. Part of St Joseph's was a grown-up girls' school and I used to exchange holy pictures with a tiny homesick German baroness, a lost and lonely boarder.

This was the moment chosen by Pope Pius for the reintroduction into the Church of child Communion. Until then lay adults were happy to make an Easter Communion and about three others in the course of the year, while children were confirmed and made their first Communion between thirteen and fifteen. Heavens, the fuss! We were all to be little saints; we must all know the Catechism by heart (I still do) we must never again sin, we must never lie down to sleep without putting ourselves in imagination 'within our coffins at the feet of our crucified Saviour'. It was that I suppose which started me off on a lifetime of shrieking nightmares from which I have never recovered. After the first one my mother bent over my bed saying, 'Nonsense, darling, the room is full of angels not coffins', and as she went out of the room she muttered to herself – and it was strange to hear those words on my mother's lips – 'Those nuns! I'd like to strangle some of them.'

By the time our First Communion came round we were all in a state of ferment. We had had a special message from the Pope. Carrie and my cousin Minnie had new dresses. I had a dreadful sailor suit, not with trousers but with knickers, not with a knotted cord but with a white silk bow. I was a German nun's dream of Bill Benbow. Our minds were chockablock with miracles; every time we went to Benediction I expected to see

Our Blessed Lord step out of the monstrance. I occasionally rehearsed what I would say when it happened.

Like Napoleon – though I resemble him in little else – I have never forgotten the day of my First Communion. That night Carrie and I and Minnie the cousin, Auntie Midge's daughter, slept in the convent, a great event, with a nun sleeping behind closed curtains at the end of the room. Mother, I learned many years later, had insisted either on that, or no First Communion. 'You always were a nervous frightened child, dear.' Minnie wept all night – she was a nervous frightened child too – and in the morning there was the horror of the sailor suit to be faced rather than the splendid reality of the Sacrament. We had been rehearsed and over-rehearsed. The actor in some of us had already taken the place of the saint.

Minnie giggled as we knelt in our places, a huge candle (as yet unlighted) before each child, all our parents in row upon row behind us, all the nuns, all the grown-up girls, the altar a blaze of light. At the right moment we went in single file to the rails, about twenty little girls, all in white dresses, veils over their heads, wreaths – and one small boy in a sailor suit, feeling his years. We received Holy Communion and returned to find our candles lighted before each one of us little temples. We made our thanksgivings for the full quarter of an hour we had been taught, and went to the first and greatest of Holy Communion childrens' breakfasts. Everyone gave us presents, mostly *Gardens of the Soul* in leather, or *Keys of Heaven* in white ivory bindings. Uncle Tom gave my first *Missale Romanum* and Auntie Agnes was there, sober.

I didn't know about poor, poor Agnes in those days. She greatly disliked children, 'but didn't mind Kevin', so that was all right with me. What a lot Auntie Agnes suffered. Cancer, both breasts amputated, endless unskilled radium applications, always drunk, so they said, but I never knew a word about that until she had been dead for years. The last I saw of her was at Uncle Tom's. There she was lying dead with a handkerchief over her face, and Uncle Tom removing the handkerchief and shining, especially for me, a shilling torch on to her face. 'Dear, oh dear' said my mother, when I told her this. But Uncle Tom did it all over again before they screwed down the coffin. You learn to keep quite close to death all your life if you've been started at a convent.

We were all confirmed, and in childish voices, renounced the world, the flesh and the Devil, as our godparents had done on our behalves at our christenings. Of course all of us little Catholics had been baptised when we were between twenty-four and thirty-six hours old.

We were confirmed at night, and by a cardinal, but I wanted to feel the Holy Ghost descend on me as Cardinal Bourne laid his hands on my head. It was a disappointing evening and no one gave us presents that time. But the next morning I arose a soldier of Christ, a being filled with the Holy Spirit. You can never quite lose that no matter how hard you try.

The year after my first Holy Communion I gave up reading for Lent, because it was what I liked best. That was the year of the *Titanic* disaster, of the introduction by Mr Lloyd George of his Ninepence for Fourpence insurance schemes (my father at once became chairman of something called The Westminster Catholic Insurance Society), and of the longest summer holiday of my life, apart from that steady preparation for the grave called retirement. What I wanted to know about the *Titanic* was whether the ship reached the bottom as a ship, or like a tray flattened by the pressures which Harmsworth's *Popular Science* told me made plates or ribbons of luminous deep water fish. We had no sense of tragedy at the loss of life.

To give up reading for Lent was an idea of my own. Like so many other of my 'abandonments' through life, it failed. I broke down somewhere about Laetare Sunday, that mid-Lent occasion on which the priest, if he has them, wears pink vestments. As with all my failures, a day of guilt ensued; it was spent in reading *Helen's Babies*. Carrie had given up sweets and went triumphantly through to Easter Sunday as usual. My father that year gave up cigars, but was compelled by my mother to start smoking again after dinner on Ash Wednesday. She said that a mortification should never be permitted to dislocate the entire house.

It was a serious business in those days, being a little Catholic. There were cribs to be made at Christmas and little altars for Our Lady to be kept decked with flowers all through the month of May. There were Acts of Mortification and Offerings Up of Disappointments to be made daily. There were compulsive sharings of treasures, there was the perpetual inculcation of the belief that if you really want it, it is probably wrong for you to have it. 'Bumpkin sacraments', as David Jones called them, 'are for the young time'. Perhaps they are no bad preparation for the later times and the essential, the compulsory, 'giving up'. There were, too, all those acts of contrition, all those childish confessions. 'Pray Father Bless me, for I have sinned.' Sin has gone out now, along with Hell and Eternal Damnation, but there was a lot of sin about in 1910, and a lot of anguish engendered by the endlessness of endlessness. Nuns were very good at measuring the infinite in terms of clock time. 'Imagine a great desert, all sand as far as the eye can reach. And a little bird. Every thousand years that little bird flies to that desert and flies away with a single grain of sand in his beak. And when all the desert has gone, taken away by the little bird at the rate of one grain every thousand years, not one second of eternity will have passed.'

My mother would have none of it. 'We shall understand it all when we get there. And of course Hell won't last for ever. In any case there isn't such a place, dear. I could never believe in our Blessed Lord, as I do, *and* in Hell. That wouldn't make sense.' All the same, every Saturday, round about six o'clock, there I was. 'Pray, Father, bless me for I have sinned.' And I really thought I had. Perhaps I had; I certainly have since.

Around Easter that year there began to be murmurings and uneasiness in the house. Something might be the matter with Netta, my eldest sister. She was really grown up, big and incredibly beautiful, back from school in France, discontented, full of strange theories about the Fact of Reality, the Meaning of Meaning, the Contemplative Life, the Life of Good Works, the Need for Self Abnegation, the Desire and Pursuit of the Whole. 'Am I here?' she would cry out to my mother. And Mother would say, 'I know you're here, dear.' Netta longed to be like St Martin. She would fling her coat about the shoulders of beggar women – but she wanted a new coat from my father next morning. She would press her weekly golden sovereign into the hands of some poor cripple, but another sovereign had to be found. She did not, as far as I remember, wheel strange and hideously diseased babies into the house, as my sister Carrie was

27

later to do, but like Carrie – like most young Catholic girls – she felt that sooner or later her life must be Given to God. There was a French order of nuns in London, the Nuns of the Cenacle, and to these Netta went frequently. There began to be a pining away. Dr Muir was called in and talked of consumption. My father remembered the Scourge of Ireland, and that all his relatives had died of tuberculosis. Three of his children had died at Grange Lodge. He began feverishly to build a sunroom for Netta on to the back of Desmond Cottage. It was also becoming time for 'Kevin to sleep alone; after all, dear, Carrie is two years older.' So a little bedroom, with a jutting-out leaded window, was under construction for Kevin.

It was a belief of my father's that he should have been a carpenter. By this he meant being an architect engaged on gigantic building projects throughout the world. Of course he could design a sun bedroom for Netta, a tiny bedroom for Kevin, and a huge sitting room beneath. This should have french windows and side windows and should lead out to a mosaic extension of the original small mosaic hall; it should be, in my father's words, 'an, how shall I put it, an adjunct, a rounding off, an embellishment, a turning of a cottage into a house, a place to live'. My father never made one word do if he could think of a dozen – and he always could.

So what with the builders being driven insane by his constant supervision, Mother finding Netta too much, Netta's health apparently beginning to fail, her sunroom unlikely to get completed for months – or for years unless my father was kept away – it was decided that we must all go away. Who decided? I can make a very good guess. The place chosen was Broadstairs, and there my father 'took' a large house standing in a big garden. It was about five hundred yards from the sea, and close to the house sometimes considered to be the original of Bleak House. Bella was to come with us and so was Mrs Tomasi's daughter.

Every moment of our journey there will be with me while life remains. In later years, all members of the family would go to any lengths to avoid travelling anywhere with my father. A bus trip with him in London could be an experience biting into the soul like acid into marble. He knew the number and the route of every bus from Piccadilly Circus to the wilds of Essex. He knew the train services from every here to every there. He knew that the 8.16 from Radlett connected with some forgotten service out of Kentish Town which joined a slow train to Broadstairs on the old South Eastern and Chatham line out of Holborn, or Crofton Park, or God knows where. Not for my father the comfortable journey from Radlett to St Pancras, the cab to Victoria, the smooth run into Thanet.

It took us all day and everything went wrong. My father travelled first class; Bella, with the invalid Netta, travelled second; Mother, with Carrie and me and Mrs Tomasi's daughter, were in the hard-backed third-class carriages of the time. There was, of course, neither train nor connection of any sort at Kentish Town. There we all sat on the uninspiring station while my father, foaming and raving, interrogated a porter. I can see the porter still; in those days they were sticklers for the uniforms of the lines to which they belonged. This was a Midland man, neat, carrying, as porters always seemed to be carrying in those days, an oily lamp and a handful of cotton waste. He knew and cared nothing for the South Eastern and Chatham railway. He left my father standing alone, and us a frightened, huddled group. It was early in the day still, about nine o'clock I suppose. We had been out of Radlett perhaps an hour.

Some time before lunch we arrived at a station so improbable that I hestitate to name it. Can it have been one of the Hams, East or West? I shall never now discover how we arrived there. By that time Netta had ceased to know us, a technique she was often to employ over the years. She had become a young lady travelling with her maid, and not even a glance from her was directed at the two already filthy children with their slatternly worn-out mother, a pile of trunks, and a frantic servant trying not to be frightened of the raging bearded man, who was damning George Stephenson and all his works to a hastily summoned station master.

The journey went on and on. Twenty years or so later I spent a blissful year alone with my mother in our Irish house. She filled in a few gaps, shuddering from time to time. It seems that my father had 'reserved a compartment' but his elaborate arrangements to join it en route had broken down from the start and we never caught up with it as it travelled empty from wherever it started towards Broadstairs. It was the knowledge that he was paying twice and getting nothing which produced an apoplectic father, a resigned mother, an aloof Netta, and a pair of distressed and bewildered children being comforted and scolded by an Italian-Cockney girl half out of her mind.

It was a hot day and somewhere amid the second-class grandeur of the final dreadful train Netta ordered Bella to bring her a cooling drink. I was never a crying child; I have been told that I was that most frightening of infants for all parents, a silent, wide-eyed, observing child. I saw Bella Macdonald arrive at our compartment, heard her Scottish voice outlining the clan history of the Macdonalds, their hatred of servitude, their readiness to be martyred, if necessary even by Campbells, rather than bow down in the house of Rimmon. The Campbells always came into Bella's tirades. If I didn't hear it all that day, I heard it often enough, and knew it all by heart. My resigned mother certainly did. 'Now Bella dear, she doesn't mean it. We're going away because she's not strong. Think of poor Minnie, Bella dear.' Mother knew as well as anyone how to play a trump at the right moment. Bella in tears rushed away for a glass of water. She had loved my sister Minnie, dead, so young and beautiful, at fourteen.

We got to Broadstairs, and – believe it or not – my father suggested a walk to the new house from the station. Suddenly my mother was all fire and ice. 'A cab, and the luggage with us, not collected by a boy for a shilling in the morning. All that, *now*, this moment, or I go away *now* and leave you all.' That was the first time I actually heard the words I was to hear so often over the years, and which my elder brothers, and Netta, must already have heard over and over again. 'A cab now, Fitz, or I shall run away for ever and beg my bread from door to door. I must have done something terribly wrong as a girl to have brought all this upon myself.' My father was wax in Mother's hands; she knew exactly when to stop putting up with things. A cab was called, the luggage – round-topped trunks – loaded on to the roof, all of us stuffed inside and off we went. But not the first-class passenger. A lordly figure, with top hat, umbrella, black coat, and striped trousers, he walked. When we were all safely inside, he paid the cabman his fare and gave him a cigar as a tip. He preferred to offer a half-crown Havana, which no one wanted, to 'demeaning a fellow human being with offers of money for rendered personal services'. But being demeaned always seemed to be what they wanted.

That was a wonderful summer in Broadstairs. Every morning Nora Tomasi took us to the beach and if she had time to spare Mother joined us for a little while towards midday. There were the cliffs and Dumpton Gap, Uncle Mack's Broadstairs Minstrels, the strange banjo-shaped pier, the gigantic horse who drew the bathing machines out to sea, the paddling in black and white check rubber paddling drawers, the shrimping, the crowds, the picnics.

Uncle Mack's Minstrels were the champion beach concert party of that year. Every morning, blacked up, in blue blazers and white flannel trousers, the minstrel troupe moved along the beach, banjos strumming, collecting boxes rattling, each man in a straw hat bearing his name. Uncle Mack, Uncle Harry, Uncle Tom, Uncle Ben and Uncle Arthur. In the afternoons, they gave us a proper show from a platform on the beach, with deck chairs at threepence and sixpence. At these Uncle Harry sang tear-jerking melodies in a light tenor voice, while shredding large squares of cunningly folded paper into intricate lace patterns. The set-up on the stage was the formal arrangement of all minstrel shows. Two corner men, Mr Bones and Mr Interlocutor, a serious Uncle at the harmonium, Uncle Mack (banjo always humming) moving about stage managing, a heavy comic, and a light comedian. Every afternoon, there was a competition for children and one day I stepped forward and announced that I would like to sing.

My little treble voice sang Uncle Mack's winning hit of the moment:

> I'm Henery the Eighth I am!
> Henery the Eighth I am, I am!
> I got married to the widow next door,
> She's been married seven times before.
> Every one was a Henery,
> She wouldn't have a Willie or a Sam;
> I'm her eighth old man called Henery,
> I'm Henery the Eighth I am.

I was told to stand aside. This meant I was in the running for a prize. 'Please show by your applause which little girl or boy you favour. This little boy? This little boy? This lovely little girl? This little boy?' I won second prize, a penknife with two blades. One side was inscribed, 'Always read *Tit-Bits*', the other, '*Tit-Bits* every week'. My brother Tom took the knife away; Tom was fifteen and I was too young for it, but I didn't mind. I walked on air for a day or two, an artist in the making, and decided to try again, and this time to win first prize.

It was not to be. Uncle Mack knew a great deal too much about business to allow the same child to win two prizes in a week, thus alienating every other mother and nursemaid in the audience. I was due to be humbled, and humbled I was. 'And what is it to be today, my fine upstanding concert artist?' 'Please, Uncle Mack, I thought I'd like to sing "Any Old Iron?"' 'Oh, you did, did you? We can't have "Any Old Iron?" sung by any old artist. The part needs skill, it needs props. Uncle Ben, kindly step forward and array our promising young friend.' By the time I was allowed to sing I had been loaded, amidst the sadistic laughter of every nurse and mother who had been present at my Henery the Eighth triumph, with the top hat, the green waistcoat, the huge watch chain that 'went' with the song when Uncle Ben sang it. Then I was pushed forward.

> Any old iron, any old iron?
> Any any any old iron?
> You look neat, talk about a treat!
> You look dapper, from your topper to your feet,
> Dressed in style, grand new tile,
> Your father's old red tie on,
> But I wouldn't give you tuppence
> for your old watch chain,
> Old iron, old iron.'

My voice faded into tears, I flung off the clothes and slunk from the stage, unapplauded, and unprized. 'They never gave him a chance,' said Bella.

Our picnics in Dumpton Gap were fun. We started early, paddled on the receding tide and, at last, could walk round the cliff foot and home along the Broadstairs sands. One lovely day Mother undressed me and put me into my little slip; I splashed about for a while and came back to be dried and dressed. In the middle of all that a woman walked over and said to Mother: 'You should be ashamed to display a naked man-child on a public beach.' The whole family leapt to 'action stations', Bella on her feet, Nora Tomasi getting ready to strike, Netta searching for the right phrase. Mother was first, as always. 'You will never come to any harm, dear lady, if you never see anything worse than my little son with his clothes off.' The dear lady went speechless away.

Once when the tide was going out I paddled by myself round the cliff foot and into Dumpton Gap. I had seen boys climbing on the low Broadstairs cliff faces and I thought I would try. Soon I was in great difficulty at, I now suppose, some ten to fifteen feet off the ground. I was frightened and very much alone on an illimitable cliff at an enormous height. I must have whimpered because a young man reading a book underneath me looked up. 'Stay quite still,' he said, climbed up to me, took me on his back and climbed down. I thought of him nearly half a century later on Snowdon. There was a whimper and a shriek from above me coming out of thick fog and I heard myself calling out 'Stay quite still.' That was my first and only mountain rescue, a pretty young woman, flat on her face in the far gulley of the summit zigzags, frightened silly. I knew the feeling; I was a member of the Climbers' Club by then.

The horse and the bathing machines were the sight I liked best at Broadstairs. There was no mixed bathing in those days, and women seemed to put on even more clothes when they went into the water than they wore on land. At certain times of the day and tide it was 'Ladies' Hour'. Those who were going to bathe entered the machines on the shore side, shut themselves in, and performed their mysteries. Then, one by one, the machines were dragged into the sea, the great horse breasting the waves, led by a heroic figure in oilskins. Far out to sea – several yards I suppose – an elderly woman in rubber clothing stood with the sea to her armpits, rocking to the swell and extending friendly arms to the ladies who emerged, shrieking and holding back, from the seaward doors of the machines. The bathing ladies were closely covered from neck to ankle in loose-fitting garments trimmed with gay braid. No suggestion of the female form was revealed even when the garment became wet. But I was used to shapeless females. I was a convent child. It was the horse I wanted never to miss, and hardly ever did. Adult bathing direct from the beach was strictly forbidden. For men, the machines were pulled a little farther out; the men wore skirted garments with blue and white circles and were greeted in the water by a man.

King George V was crowned in June 1911. Just as for my first Communion it was arranged that Carrie and I should stay at the convent because my parents 'had seats' and, on top of that, had been married for twenty-five years. The Coronation is imprinted upon my mind for two reasons. My mother had given me a bound volume of *Chums* for my birthday, June 19th, and my godmother had sent me an enormous birthday cake, with my name and lots of good wishes all iced into it. Both went with me to the convent. The head girl borrowed *Chums,* and kept it until I went home; the nun in charge of Juniors took the cake and divided it into the number of pieces that she had children. 'There must sharing always be' she said, as I carried my huge cake round the tea table in the refectory. I did get a slice.

My parents never had a honeymoon. Mother told me, long after this, that the night before the wedding my father had come to tell her that a friend of his was hideously down on his luck and had to have fifty pounds. That was the sum my father had put aside for the honeymoon and he asked Mother what to do. She said to me: 'I knew there couldn't be a blessing on our marriage if we kept that money so I told your father to give it to his friend.' 'Did he ever pay it back,' I asked. 'No, dear,' she said.

That generous, warm-hearted side of my father was one half of him. But the other half was never far away. As he walked to the wedding, Uncle Tom told me, he realised that he ought to have a newer pair of gloves. Cotton gloves, as then worn at weddings, were about a shilling a pair and he turned into a haberdasher's. Shops in those days were often compartmented by screens jutting out from the counters. From behind one of those my Uncle Tom heard a well-known voice like a cathedral organ. It was the bridegroom engaged in a last-moment purchase of socks. 'And what reduction will you make for quantity?' the voice said. 'Suppose I take a quarter dozen?'

34

That was the other side, the side that was to scar me for life. I was sent at the age of twelve into a shop for boys in Holborn to say to an assistant: 'I think my father will buy me that dressing gown if you reduce the price to eighteen shillings.' He had already been beaten down from the level pound.

It was a dreadful experience to eat out – or indeed to go anywhere – with my father, and all of us – even my mother – avoided it whenever possible. I have sat with my father in restaurants while a special price for half-portions was negotiated with the management. I have sat on the tops of buses with him while the obvious shortcomings and general mental decay of the stranger in the next seat were freely adumbrated. I have been with him when to my horror he has opened the garden gate, walked up the path, peered in at some happy family at supper, and turned away commenting, in a thunderous murmur; 'Typically shiftless, typically shiftless.'

Two

Early in 1911, as I sat in the topmost branches of a tree in the garden, a voice from below called out: 'Would you come down for a moment? I want to talk to you.' It came from a lady whom I knew only by sight. I was already only too well accustomed to the female thumb – Mother's, Sister Emerentia's, Netta's, Bella's, Nora Tomasi's, many, many others. So I obediently came down from the tree and went across the road to Mrs Vaughan's house, where I met Mrs Vaughan's little boy. Years later I learned that Mrs Vaughan had called on my mother the same day, describing me as 'a little boy with the most beautiful manners'. That was why little boys were sent to convents. They learnt in them much to wreck their lives, much to regret, but you can be sure that such little boys will be everlastingly getting up to open doors for Mother Superior, classroom nuns, little girls. They will never be able to sit in a bus or train while a strong and much healthier woman stands.

The little boy I played with that afternoon was different from anyone I had ever met before. He had shiny fair hair, and a couple of prominent teeth, but what made him different was a capacity for total absorption in what he was doing – and what he was doing was always something utterly strange to me and to my whole nature. A year or two before I met him I had gone through the routine business of playing with trains. This meant being provided with a circle of rails, a clockwork engine, and three trucks. You wound up the engine and, holding the key with your thumb to prevent the thing starting, you put the apparatus on to the rails, let go, and watched it run off on to the carpet. After a while you put it away in its box and went back to *The Swiss Family Robinson* or *Coral Island*. It would be marvellous, you thought, to ride on an ostrich, or to be able to swim and dive and be taken down like Peterkin to a cave under the sea. 'A strange child,' you heard people saying, 'always sitting about with a book. So unhealthy.'

36

My way wasn't at all the way George Vaughan played with trains. He was six months younger than I, but light-years older when it came to trains. There he was, on that first day, crouched on the floor with an immense railway system filling the room about him. There were tunnels and stations, there were porters and passengers, there were scale models of the Midland express locomotives. They were started, stopped, or put into reverse by push-buttons in the driving cabs. The rails ran under sofas and armchairs, there were intricate sidings, there were signals which could be made to glow red or green. There were buffer stops against which accurate models of different kinds of wagon could be shunted.

From the beginning of our acquaintance he tended to say: 'Hold this a minute', or 'Keep blowing through this while I get the end fixed.' As the years went by it was to be: 'If you put that book down a second you could come over here and steady this jack', or: 'You wouldn't be in this sort of mess if you stuck to one woman; look at me.' He has been a lifelong friend and a teacher of strange mysteries. He is not going to think very highly of the funeral arrangements made for me when that time eventually comes. 'No system, no proper rehearsal,' he'll be saying as someone stumbles with the coffin on the walk to the graveside.

At nine and a half he was unbeatable as a railway manager. And unlike me he called his father 'Father'. The first words I heard him say as Mrs Vaughan took me into his company were: 'If you wouldn't mind moving your leg, Father, I thought of laying a bit of track where it is.' Mr Vaughan moved his leg and smiled at me. I was in; I was part of the family.

By this time Bella had been sacked. Heavens, what a scene that was, with trunks being thrown down the stairs and my mother adamant, because at last she scented freedom from a tyranny that had begun with the birth of my eldest brother Will and had never ceased. Bella always treated Mother, Netta and my eldest brother as though they were in prams. Carrie she didn't like and ignored. She spoiled me. I took her back to nannydom. It was after me that she was kept on and grew into a general servant of tremendous power. She wrote to me for the rest of her life but not to anyone else. She never forgave Mother and Mother never forgave her. But what it was that each was

not forgiving the other for would take a long time to explain.
I had left the convent now. What was to be the next step,
what should the child be prepared for? Heaven, of course, but
already he'd been conditioned about that. A proper little boy's
school must be thought about, a preparatory school. In the
meantime there was Mrs Pillans giving lessons in the new
bungalow up the hill. And Mrs Pillans, 'with that difficult
eccentric husband, poor woman', was a Catholic.

So every morning up to Mrs Pillans I went. I thought nothing
of arithmetic, and less of all the other nonsense she tried to teach
me. Rubbishy stories about bears and fairies, picture books
about King Pippin, *Books for the Bairns*, in pink paper covers,
and *First Steps* in This and That for Tiny Tots. What I looked
forward to every day was the elderly gentleman sitting with a
book or a scribbling pad in a corner of the teaching room. He
was said to be something quite frightful – an atheist and, what
was worse in the eyes of Radlett, he never went to work or ran
for trains. He went for long walks by himself, always with a
camera, and took beautiful pictures which he hung on the walls
of his house. One day he spoke to me while I was looking at one
of them: 'Taste's the thing,' he said. And of course he was right.

We became friends and I was very fond of him. The scrib-
blings I noticed when I first knew him were *Tales from the
Arabian Nights,* a children's book he was doing as a bit of
hackwork. 'Burton's the man for you, Kevin, but that will
come later; there's a lot of this stuff that's not fit for young
people, or come to that, old men like me. And there's a same-
ness about the Muslim world that very quickly palls. Try looking at a Turkish carpet all day long and you'd soon go mad. But
you'll find all this out for yourself, Kevin.'

In the autumn of 1919, in Ireland, I was sent a copy of the
Radlett local paper. It contained a fierce attack on Mr Pillans and
I learnt then what conservative Radlett really thought about the
radical atheist in its midst. I sat down and wrote my first letter
to a newspaper. I was seventeen and a half and was still unaware
that there is nothing so dangerous as the public defence of a
friend. They printed my letter and everyone in Radlett said,
'That nice FitzGerald boy has been infected by that wicked old
man.' But I never heard him mention politics or politicians,
religion or the lack of it, God or His absence from the heavens.

We used to go for long walks in school holidays and talked of books and pictures and of taste; of music, of the habits of animals and of men, of trying to be self-contained. He was a very good man.

It was while with Mrs Pillans that I took an unfortunate step on a downward path. There was a farmer in Radlett called Farmer Smith, and he had a daughter, reserved and beautiful and trained as a teacher and games mistress. She used to come to Mrs Pillans 'to play with the children and to teach them simple games'. *That's* what I should have resisted, should have wanted to resist, should have been encouraged to resist. But the dreadful destructive 'games' virus was injected into me, unresisting, by Miss Smith. Under her delightful aegis, I learned the old English game of stoolball, and learnt also to kick a small version of an association football. I was to be useless at these pursuits and always to loathe them, but the damage was done. It was Miss Smith who did it. It was the seed she had sown that led me to captain Stafford and play Rugby football for Staffordshire, when I might have been spending whole glorious summers in the Alps. But I loved her dearly, a good solid useful early love. It was Miss Smith's bosom which was the first bosom to dwell in my innocent mind.

George Vaughan was no pupil of Mrs Pillans. He went daily by train to Finchley Road Station, thence to Frognal and the new tube station of Hampstead. Exactly across the road from the tube station was Holly Hill, and the first big house on Holly Hill – a high wall about it, a green door in the wall with a polished brass plate carrying a shield with oak leaves and acorns and a Latin motto 'Paulatim' – was the Preparatory Branch of University College School. And to that, because George Vaughan went to it, and for that one and only reason, I was sent. And what a place it was!

When my mother's dearest friend died, her husband took to the bottle and was found dead in a street near his house, a week after the funeral. Mrs Carroll had been a woman of infinite kindness, so it was no wonder he felt her loss. She never came to see us at Grove Lodge without loading herself with presents, and the memory of that happy practice, which had always worried my mother, now caused her to put an end to birthdays. 'There are lots of us,' she used to say, 'and if people have to remember exactly when we were all born and give us presents there won't be a month in the year for them free from expense.'

It was thus quite difficult for me to remember my date of birth when Mr Simmons, the Headmaster of UCS Prep, asked me for it the day my father took me there to be enrolled. But if I could not remember my birthday I can remember Mr Simmons very clearly. I have since met a large number of Balliol men, but Mr Simmons was the first. I judge them all by him; do they come up to his standard? Scholarly, urbane, a trifle unworldly, he had a conviction that all boys, and by that he meant every boy in his school, was filled with moral earnestness, a desire to better the whole world, to lead a good life, to *matter*.

The two men stood there and looked at each other, Mr Simmons in his black alpaca jacket, my father, as always on occasions he deemed of importance, top-hatted and frock-coated. They could hardly have looked more different but there was at once a sympathy between them. Mr Simmons handed me a book and invited me to read a paragraph to him. He asked me about arithmetic. Then he said these momentous words: 'We teach boys their own living language before attempting the inculcation of the dead ones, Latin and Greek.' 'Excellent,' said my father, 'it is clear that the boy will be in good hands.' 'We shall be happy to have him,' Mr Simmons said. And so it was arranged.

We were divided into houses, named after flowers. Vaughan was in 'Daffodil', but I was in 'Tulip' and came under Miss Fuller, one of the great influences of my life. I thought she was fairly old, and she must have been at least thirty. She wore the grey coat and skirt, the skirt just clearing the ground and quite full, which all women seemed to wear in those days; her hair was scraped back in a schoolmistressy way; she always spoke to us as if were shortly to be entrusted with the responsibility of governing our country. We adored her. One of us brought her flowers every day and we longed for it to be our turn for Miss Fuller to ask us to do something or other for her, to fetch a book, sweep up some rubbish, run and see if Miss Aird was still in the playground.

Miss Aird was what would be called nowadays 'dedicated' or perhaps 'committed'. She had so Scottish an accent, always calling boys 'byes', that it could sometimes be quite difficult to understand what she was saying. But it was always on the highest possible plane. We should try and be Galahads, living pure and holy lives, principally for others. We should be tolerant but firm, we should listen to good music, never read trash, search out and stand before great pictures, be serious.

Mr Simmons dominated every scene. He would sweep into a classroom, take a pile of cut, ruled paper, massage it into a fan of loose sheets, see that every boy had a sheet of paper before him, and begin. 'Let us have dictionary practice,' he would say. 'Everyone write down the word "oblation", give its meaning and add ten words all ending in "ation" which might be linked together.' There would also be days, ghastly for me, where he would begin: 'Mental arithmetic, the stretching of minds. Let us take a number, 54839. Let the first boy to double that in his head put up his hand.' Up would go Abrahams' hand, 'Please sir, 109678, sir.' 'Very good, Abrahams, but remember you have what is called a flair for that kind of thing. Any boy like to tell me the meaning of "flair"?' Sometimes he would have a book in his hand and then, sheer delight, we would hear his performances of the *Uncle Remus* stories.

There were no punishments at UCS. We were expected to behave, and we did. Minor breaches of conduct led to the issuing of 'report cards', which told against the general position of House Tulip in the terminal analysis of behaviour. But there was one grave sanction, 'The Black Book'. If your offence was so great that it smelled to heaven your name was entered into the Black Book and was written out on a card which had to be seen and countersigned by a parent or guardian. I only got one in my four years at UCS, and it was the only time in my whole life that I ever saw my father in a state of uncontrollable laughter.

My Black Book card read: 'For saying "Damn" after Pegram had stuck a nib into him.' Pegram got one too, of course. His read: 'For sticking a nib into FitzGerald and making him say "Damn".' I don't know what Pegram's father said. Mine was in bed, and he laughed and laughed, and signed the card. Then he said, 'Never do anything much worse than that, my son, and you'll be all right.'

My father in bed reminded me of the picture of Mr Pickwick

trapped in the bedroom of the middle-aged lady at the Great White Horse in Ipswich. I had not then read the book but liked seeing Mr Pickwick in his nightcap and nightshirt peering from the curtains of the bed. My father had just taken to a nightcap and continued to wear one for the rest of his life. He never wore pyjamas, 'instruments of restriction, irritation and inconvenience' he called them. His nightshirts were all 'smocked' in scarlet thread.

At UCS I felt at home. At home – my other home – the opinions of all men and all women were considered to be of value; their religious beliefs were of the first importance but their own personal affair and always worthy of respect; a serious mind was everything and a flippant approach to life nothing. That was exactly the atmosphere at UCS. The whole school had been founded to encourage toleration, to demonstrate that Jews and Catholics, Methodists and High Anglicans all had a place in English life and culture. Our school song had nothing about a breathless hush in the old school close, but much about those earnest hearts in 'the old time, the morning time, who laid intolerance low'. We lapped it up.

To this day I can remember Mr Simmons talking for an hour about Wordsworth looking at a daisy and finding that he was really looking at a silver shield with a golden boss. That led him on, in his Balliol way, to shields, to armoured knights in medieval warfare, to recognition signals, heraldry, Blue Dragons Pursuivant, and heaven knows what. There are worse ways of picking up information. When later on, in the intellectual wasteland of my Catholic public school, I discovered, one after another, some of the poets, I would let the mind run as his did and was sometimes able to get inside their heads. But Sister Emerentia, whom I visited regularly, was disturbed. She feared for my soul on seeing in my satchel *Stories from Wagner*. He was an immodest man who lived a pagan life. She thumbed through my dangerous soul-destroying text book, and all too soon came to the illustration for *Tannhauser*. There he was in the Venusberg, on his knees contemplating the goddess, who was reasonably clothed but certainly not overdressed. Sister Emerentia read out the caption; 'Oh Queen, oh Goddess, let me fly.' Then she tore out the picture. 'From the eyes, always, the immodest pictures keep, Kevin,' she said.

I told Miss Fuller about Sister Emerentia, and I told Miss Aird. Miss Fuller thought that nothing could or should influence a balanced mind and Miss Aird gave a Scottish smile in total silence. I never told anyone else. The following Monday Miss Fuller said: 'I've brought you a little present, FitzGerald.' It was the Nelson sevenpenny *Rupert of Hentzau*. 'I heard you talking about *The Prisoner of Zenda*', Miss Fuller said, 'and I knew you ought to have this.'

We were taught French by phonetics. We were all encouraged to use phonetics whenever we could, and there were certain nasty little prigs who used to send Mr Simmons phonetic postcards. As I have never been able to understand any phonetic symbols I left UCS knowing one sentence of French. It said that Monsieur Pascal cut the bread with a big knife.

In the year before the war, there burst upon us a brash, yellow-haired young master with a Cockney accent, Mr Robinson. He was to introduce a brand new and wonderfully exciting subject, Science. When he had been a week in the school I got myself removed from the top lunch table, and sat instead with the group who clustered round Mr Robinson. I can hear him still. 'Well, you can read all that tripe if you like, but I shouldn't. Get hold of *Robbery under Arms* by a chap called Ralph Boldrewood. You'll like that.' Or he would say: 'Well, it's easy. You pump the air out of something; that something is going to feel the air outside pressing on it. Tell you what, I'll have a vacuum pump with me tomorrow and we will suck the air out of things and see what happens to them.'

Heavens, how we fought to sit near Mr Robinson. And his classes were just the same. 'Gather round me and help to spill mercury all over the place; we're going to make a barometer.' 'Any of you lot know how to float a needle on water?' 'Let's make some oxygen and burn the place to the ground.'

We kept games in their places at UCS. We played association football in the winter. I got into the first eleven almost at once as an outside left and it seemed to me a lonely place. I was always thinking about death as I trotted up and down waiting for passes. I suppose that was the nuns. But games were not a part of the higher tolerant life, still less were they outlets for our lusts and frustrations. We had no lusts or frustrations. We had our black and red ringed caps, and our black and red ringed jerseys.

That meant that all who saw us knew that we were UCS boys, the advance guard of a new world. We behaved with decorum in the streets, we offered our seats to ladies in tubes and buses, we removed our caps to practically everyone. But if we were George Vaughan we carried a knife in our stocking to protect us in trains from the rough boys who went to Haberdashers at Cricklewood. Going home from UCS was the danger time. We had to wait twenty minutes at Hendon until the arrival of our train for Radlett. That was always a difficult twenty minutes for me. Sometimes our red and black ringed caps would be thrown into the paths of Manchester expresses, roaring through, sometimes we would be made to put our pennies into the 'Try Your Strength' machine so that the Haberdashers boys could try their strength. They often got our pennies back but always went on until they were finally lost.

We thought the Haberdasher boys very rough, but of course they weren't. They never hit us, only threw our caps in front of expresses, taught us to turn halfpennies into pennies by putting them on the line, and sometimes if the compartment between Hendon and Elstree was empty, which mercifully it seldom was, they would put us into the rack. That was all. Vaughan soon got the measure of them; he began to carry a chisel with his Swiss knife. They never touched him after the first time he took it out from under his jersey and they saw he meant to use it.

I was softer material and could be worked upon easily. Perhaps it would have been different if my father had allowed me to be taught boxing. But he had a poor opinion of boxing; nor was I allowed to join the Scouts. To him, that would have meant lending his countenance to the Boer War, of which he had strongly disapproved. By nature I was not aggressive and until I was seventeen or eighteen I was daily outgrowing my strength. Almost anyone could twist my arm or knock me about without much personal danger. I must have been nearly twenty before I discovered that I had become big and very strong. By that time, of course, people had lost all desire to knock me about. It was bad while it lasted, and the Haberdashers boys were only a foretaste.

I was at UCS all the first autumn of the First World War and for two terms of 1915. My brother Will had gone to the war and was in camp with B Battery HAC. My brother Tom was at St Edmunds, training to become a priest. That year he was Dux of the school, and brought home more prizes than I had ever seen, with a huge silver medal for being Dux. My father assumed this to be a normal part of the school curriculum, taking no interest in my brother's vast collection of leather-bound unreadable books, but giving him for Christmas eight volumes of Montalembert's *Monks of the West*. We must have been a nightmare family for Radlett, except for my mother, who constantly observed that she 'did not know what she had done to bring all this on herself but she must have done something'. When she was on her deathbed and Tom – clenching his fists, although he had by then been a priest for over twenty years – cried out: 'Why are you in this pain, Mother?', she said the same thing: 'I must have done something, dear.'

One day, when I was about twelve, as he was leaving for the office in his silk top hat and black frock coat, my mother asked my father if he would do something for her. 'I should like you to bring me a hundred gold sovereigns in a little bag,' she said. He said he would and sure enough he brought them that evening and handed them over without any questions, merely reminding her to put them in the bedroom safe. Some weeks later, just as he was again leaving, he realised he hadn't a penny in his pocket. 'Perhaps you would lend me one of those gold sovereigns of yours, my dear,' he said. 'I will bring you another back this evening.' 'Sovereigns?' she said, 'I have no sovereigns. I can let you have some silver.' She gave him one of her famous looks, which meant she wished to hear no more. And again he asked no questions but quietly went off with the silver. We often wondered who it was she had rescued from what disgrace or disaster with those hundred gold sovereigns. Years later I asked her. 'Never mind about that now, dear,' she said. 'It was all a long time ago.'

At the end of 1914 the first soldiers came back from France, covered with mud and wearing Robinson Crusoe jackets made of goatskin. We heard of the bitter cold, and how the Germans and our soldiers had fraternised at Christmas. Mr Honeyball, from the cottages down the road, brought home a German *pickelhaube,* given to him on Christmas morning by a German soldier. The generals and politicians soon put a stop to that nonsense. The following Christmas Day (1915) saw some of the bitterest fighting of the whole war.

There began to be talk of my going away to school. Vaughan went off to Aldenham and 'Kevin had better go somewhere'. But where? All that was a merciful nine months away. There was still nearly a year more in which I was to be treated as a real person, allowed to read everything I wanted or liked, to write little essays about Roman soldiers or Sir Galahad, to find out about Swift and Goldsmith and Peter Pindar, to read *Masterman Ready* and – in the wonderful spring of 1915, lying in bed with my annual laryngitis, a great steam kettle with a two-foot spout trilling away on the fire in my little bedroom – to discover Stevenson's *New Arabian Nights*. All those delights were to count for nothing in the next four years. I was destined for a place where riding a horse was everything, and books, except those that got you into Sandhurst or 'The Shop', 'a lot of bloody silly nonsense'.

But for the next nine months I was to be in the Sixth at my preparatory school, a prefect, in the cricket eleven, someone whose strict business it was never to allow the school cap to be disgraced, never to speak or think evil of my companions, to do noble deeds not dream them all day long. Mr Simmons was strong on doing noble deeds. Our men were doing them in France, and on the great seas of the world. We sang 'Rule Britannia' without shame, we believed that death in battle was the best death of all.

I don't suppose there was a happier boy in England than Kevin FitzGerald in the spring and summer of 1915. He was finding things out all the time and was always encouraged to find things out; he listened to his father discoursing about Byron and, in that summer holiday, talked to his brother Tom about what it would be like to go away to a public school and be a real man at last. So much pleasure to look forward to, so much misery to endure when the future came!

That was a good summer holiday. I worked all through it for Farmer Smith, proudly walking through the village leading massive cartloads of wheat and driving back the empty carts, standing up in them in the approved style, the horse really knowing what to do. Vaughan was home from Aldenham and constructed a remarkable raft which we launched in a flooded quarry and actually sailed upon.

Radlett was growing. We had one of the earliest telephone numbers, Radlett 21, and most mornings my father would twist away at the handle and after a bit would say; 'Good morning, operator, Holborn 6200 please.' A few moments later he would say: 'Good morning, Emily, I'm coming on the later train.' Then he would put on his top hat, kiss my mother and walk down to the station. He regarded 'having a holiday' as almost wicked. What a proper man did was to work at what he was doing and be much better at it and know more about it than anyone else. I was having the most appalling preparation for an English public school.

In July 1915 I mournfully said goodbye to UCS Preparatory Branch, put on a school satchel for the last time, and set off for Radlett and the wartime summer holidays of those troubled times. Food was scarce and no one 'went away'; my eldest brother was in hard training on Salisbury Plain, having been commissioned out of the HAC into the Royal Horse Artillery proper.

It was perhaps unfortunate that this was one of my father's rich periods. I was not consulted about the plans for my education or I should certainly have chosen UCS Big School, as we called it in the Preparatory Branch. But it had to be a boarding school and it had to be Catholic. There was then only one possible school to which my father felt a son of his could be sent, the Oratory. This view had been confirmed by his friend Lord Denbigh, by Cardinal Bourne, the Archbishop of Westminster, and by three or four other people of importance. Getting me there would present no problems because the right people would speak for me. I looked forward to it. I know I was relieved at not being sent to Beaumont, Downside or Ampleforth; they all sounded terrible. I had a feeling that I was going to like the Oratory. It takes a long time to learn that feelings are not to be trusted.

In the '70s of the last century, John Henry, Cardinal Newman, founded the Oratory School to be a Catholic Eton. He had round him a tiny community, mostly of Tractarian converts from Oxford, and he made his friend Father John Norris the first Headmaster. The school was always to be limited to seventy boys, and they must all be of pure British descent. At the time when I was there, the public school idea was a good deal more in evidence than any of Newman's.

That first day is over sixty years away from me but I can remember almost every dreadful moment. My father, as usual, put on a top hat and frock coat for the occasion and took me to Euston in a taxi. That in itself was a grim experience, since in those days all taxi men were disgruntled and bad-tempered, because they had been used to driving horse-cabs. The machines they steered were like something out of a Heath Robinson notebook. The driver was completely unprotected except by half a dozen frieze coats, in the lowest layer of which he kept his change, unbuttoning as he went down with diminishing speed.

In the old yard of Euston station my box fell off the cab and burst open. It was the cheapest trunk obtainable from Thomas Wallis and Co of Holborn who had also supplied all the clothes in it, including a dozen stiff Eton collars, as never worn by any Oratory boy in any circumstances whatever. I had to wear them daily for half a term, being unable in any letter to my parents to convince them that Lower School boys at the Oratory wore soft collars with a gold pin under the tie. They simply could not believe it.

My father and all the porters laughed as my clothes were gathered up and put back into my Wrong Box, but I did not. The shame of those naked pants! I did not yet know how wrong were my flannel shirts nor how awful was the football outfit which even the dormitory maid who unpacked later that evening put back into the trunk with a shudder. But already something told me they were wrong. I can see the wrong socks, all neatly rolled by loving hands, now rolling about Euston forecourt while the porters split their sides.

My father when by himself always travelled first class, but not if he was with any member of the family, and I made my first trip to Birmingham New Street in a third-class compartment of the wonderful chocolate and cream coaches of the LNWR. The service and speed were much better then than now, the locomotives all burnished, the compartments spotless. There was an express service to Birmingham every hour, on the half hour. The train was never late and it took exactly two hours non-stop.

At Euston my father had given me lunch, discussing with the waiter my finnicky habits about food, and I was glad enough to escape from that into the train. Travel with my father always meant an incident. A taxi from New Street took us to the school and I had a sense of utter doom as we entered it. We were put into a waiting room – I was later to know this as 'The Hag's Room' – and after a while the Headmaster appeared. He quite obviously disliked what he saw but my father as usual was completely impervious to what anyone thought of him. His own dislike of other people he always made manifest at once. He shook the Headmaster's hand, said that he was a busy man but could spare a little time to be shown round, and we began a tour which for many years came back in sleep as a nightmare. As we walked from one dark dank building to the next, from one battered wreck of a classroom to another, and eventually arrived at the huge apartment called the Big Schoolroom, it became clearer and clearer to me that my father regarded the Headmaster, Father Edward Pereira, as what he used to describe (rather loudly as a rule) as 'a man of no account'. It was equally clear that Father Edward was of the same opinion about him. They hated each other quite soon. In the Big Schoolroom my father frowned at the mass of names carved into the panelling and said: 'A serious disfigurement.' Father Edward said: 'Money could not buy one of them', and swept us into the Little School-room. In the billiard room my father said: 'Not a game at which I would care for a son of mine to become proficient.' Father Edward said: 'By the look of him, there is no fear of that.' My father was tiring of this educational debauch and said again that he was a busy man but that he must write a letter before leaving the school. We were thankfully rushed back to the 'Hag's Room' where the 'Hag', the school Matron, Miss Gay-Smith, her long pointed nose sharpening up the austerity of her London Hospital sister's uniform, disapprovingly gave my father an envelope and some writing paper. He scribbled a note, gave me half a crown and a bearded kiss, said 'Goodbye' and there I was alone with Father Edward. He instantly called up a boy. 'This is FitzGerald,' he said. 'Show him about.' He disappeared and the boy said: 'Clear off and look after your bloody self.' I thus became an Oratory boy. I had been 'cleared off' by Lentaigne who died of wounds as a major-general in the Second War. He was a nice man but I only found that out later.

As a man grows older his sleepless nights become more frequent. It is then that the horrors of his past sins return, the unforgivable seductions, the drunken bouts at which the everlastingly unpardonable thing was said, the cheatings and lyings, the broken promises, the unfulfilled ambitions. Then, too, for me, comes back that eternity when I was 'away at school'. Sometimes between midnight and three in the morning I relive a whole endless term, seeing and naming my companions, hearing their voices, wondering all over again if the holidays will ever come.

The difference between 'justice' and 'injustice' does not lie in the facts of the case but in the viewpoints of the actors. It was right and just that Father Philip of the Oratory School should confiscate (and never return) my copy of *The Dop Doctor*. He probably thought that it was a book about drugs and would all his life remain unaware that a dop doctor is a South African medical man, overfond of Cape brandy, and that of all the boys in the school I was the one who would have profited most from that technically incompetent but deeply serious novel. The same Father Philip, then Prefect of Studies, deprived me of the prize for Catholic apologetics. 'You got all your answers from a book,' he suggested, and thought I was impertinent when I suggested that there was no other way known to me whereby to become proficient in the theological observations of St Thomas Aquinas.

I am haunted by my total unsuitability for that school, by contempt for what passed there for learning, by loathing for the parades and absurd regimentations of the OTC, by a deep dislike of the methods employed which found favour with everyone else. I was the odd man out. Everything about me was wrong. My clothes were wrong. My parents were wrong; they did not hunt and none of my forebears had been in the Coldstream. Worst of all, I did not want to know the sort of people that the others wanted to know or lead the sort of lives they wanted to lead. The school was the best Catholic school in

England. There was and is nothing like it anywhere else in the world. Newman, the Cardinal, had all the right ideas. They did not happen to suit me, and I suffered terribly. That is a carefully chosen word; my sufferings were terrible.

I suppose the first term was the worst. I could not conform because I did not know how to, not because I would not. I went home black and blue. I went home three days before the end of term because my eldest brother had been ordered to France. The Headmaster said, 'You are going home, FitzGerald, to say goodbye to a soldier, but you must return immediately; you understand that, of course.' 'Yes, sir,' I said.

My father would not let me return. 'No man in his senses', he said, 'would expect a boy to return from Radlett to Birmingham for a couple of nights. You have misunderstood the situation and the answer is "No".' Until the day I left, 'The Man', as the Headmaster at that school was always called, referred to me as 'the boy who lied his way home before the end of term'. My father regarded all that as too trivial to require explanation, even when the Headmaster wrote to set me a fearsome holiday task as a specific punishment. The Headmaster meted out justice; justice was seen to be done. But I was the victim of gross injustice. That is the way lives are affected, why sixty years later old men lie awake in the dark, sometimes sweating for their sins, but just as often resenting those twists and turns of fortune which could have been avoided and were not.

In those early days of the First World War, boys were leaving school every term who would be killed within a year. Two or three came back, armless or shot through the face, to go on with interrupted school work and preparation for universities or law chambers, or that strange place, the 'World'.

We were Oratory boys, utterly remote from those 'scarcely Catholic' boys scattered about the country in the charge of Benedictines, Jesuits and the like. No one had to spy on us, or burst unannounced into the 'lounge', where each form took its leisure. That was unfortunate for me, because I was frequently undergoing some diabolical form of torture at the hands of someone later to win a DSO with two bars. But in some odd way I always felt mentally free.

On my second day I wrote a frantic postcard to my mother asking to be taken away. She replied saying this could not be done but that she would come to see me. She came at half term and took me out to tea, at last being persuaded about soft collars, and ending six weeks of unendurable Eton-collared misery by reluctantly getting six soft collars of the wrong shape. But they helped and within a year I had the proper supply of long points and gold pins. She also brought me a cloth cap of the permitted pattern; only the highest in the school were permitted soft hats, and only then if sufficiently athletic. My wrong cap had a button on top of it. Moreover it 'matched' my overcoat. If my parents had struggled for years to think of a method of doing lasting injury to their youngest son, that was the answer which would have been provided. But I survived that, and much else. I survived knowing – and alas saying – that a mixture of manganese dioxide and potassium chlorate would, when heated in a test tube, give off the gas oxygen. I survived knowing the Catechism backwards – the nuns had done a good job on me. But I only just survived the Headmaster's remark one morning: 'FitzGerald appears to be the only boy in 3b with a faint glimmer of intelligence.' There came a whisper from behind of a boy later to win the almost standard Oratory DSO (in his case as a colonel of tanks at Alamein): 'Just wait a few minutes, FitzGerald; just a few minutes.' I knew by then exactly what that meant.

Fifty years after that dreadful day the President of the Alpine Club remarked in the course of a peaceful mountain walk that I was a civilised man. 'Where did you get all this?' he asked. My mind then and there, half way up Pen Helyg, went back to the day of 'glimmering intelligence'. Was it from the Oratory School that I should trace such civilisation as I possessed?

My experiences there should have taught me half a dozen really major lessons, a faint grasp of which would have carried me to a seat on the Woolsack, a generalship in the Army, or the chairmanship of some gigantic industrial enterprise. All I had to learn was when to give in, and to whom; when to speak and when to be silent; never to suggest to those in lawful authority over me that they were morons or to my equals that they were yahoos. I have learned all those lessons now, except the most important of all, when to give way and to whom.

Doing the right thing at the right time and in the right way and fitting into one's surroundings are civilised virtues. They are what one is supposed to learn at a public school. I was no good at any of that. But what the President of the Alpine Club meant by civilisation was something quite different. And however it was that I learnt to like the poets – and such strange ones as David Jones – it was nothing to do with the Oratory School.

At the end of my first year came the great frost of 1916. For weeks games were suspended, with all the posturings of the OTC. Instead we skated. That was bliss, pure bliss. I knew how to skate, owned a pair of Dutch runners, the old-fashioned screw-fitted wood-mounted Dutch runners of those far-off days. They brought me into the companionship of the ice, and to the discovery that I liked quite a number of Oratory boys. One of them took off his superb rink skates and lent them to me for a whole hour on the afternoon that my Dutch runners fell to pieces.

The Oratory School was also quite a good place to be on the day King George V opened the new Birmingham Children's Hospital. Merely because of my height, I was in the combined Birmingham Schools' Guard of Honour, was inspected by the King, remembered just enough drill not to become – as I normally was – entangled with my bayonet during the fixing operation, and had an absolutely perfect front-seat view of the officer in charge of us all failing to manage either himself or his horse at the sudden blast of trumpets on his command: 'Royal salute: present arms.' Those on the right of the line stood rock steady at the 'present' as our commanding officer, his horse moving backwards on two legs, mowed down the graded centre of our front rank in a confused swathe. His Majesty regarded the scene with royal aloofness and I have often wondered what he thought.

All that long day we lined the streets, someone occasionally dropping forwards or backwards in a faint. I cut preparation and went to bed when at last we returned to school. That was another black mark; I was being clever and original, I was asleep in bed instead of being asleep over a desk with the rest of the school. That demonstrated that I was not 'officer material' – a statement I had made myself to my superiors over and over again. But I should have let them find it out for themselves. I was a disastrous Oratory boy.

How I hated the compulsory games. Our association football at UCS had been geared to the rugger we should be playing when we arrived at the Big School. Here at the Oratory that absurd farce of snooker with the feet was played as the game of the school. I found myself unable to bear it. I became an unknown dreg in the third game. There was nothing lower in the school, except the summer third game of cricket. I was in that too, and I loved cricket. I love it still, but as an art form to be looked at, not as a participatory game. I have always lacked the team spirit. Perhaps, if I had been allowed to become a Boy Scout . . . But I suspect that I should have been a disastrous Boy Scout too.

There came a day when in some fit of despair on the part of someone or other I was asked if I would care to be an acolyte at the Oratory Church High Mass on Sundays. In this great church we had our private gallery, reached through a door in our private chapel, and attendance at High Mass was voluntary. The request, however, was a command and I obeyed it happily. I became an acolyte, and in due course a server. This activity brought two great pleasures into my Oratory life. With another boy I became sacristan in our own chapel, laying out vestments, marking up the Missal, taking care of all the accoutrements of Catholic worship. And I had the privilege of going into the organ loft in the Oratory church when High Mass was over to watch and hear Mr Collins playing for us after he had finished the departure voluntary. That took me out of the harsh world. The Fathers of the Oratory have never wasted the time of their congregations with hours of boring Gregorian plain chant or the harsh Ignatian simplicities of the Jesuits. Under the ceremonial mastership of Father Denis Sheil High Mass at the Birmingham Oratory often lasted more than two hours. It was never long enough for me, which led to the strange belief of the Hag that it was my fixed intention to enter a contemplative order of monks. But in the end I was a disappointment even to the Hag. She liked me enough to confer upon me one of the great honours the school had to bestow, a request for my photograph when I was leaving. I had it specially taken, and sent her a copy. But she did not know my father, and had not grasped his views on how much should be spent on what. 'You are the only boy', read her letter of thanks, 'who, asked for a photograph, has sent it to me on a postcard.'

The Battle of Jutland gave us a strange night at the Oratory School. We were at preparation when the newsboys were heard crying along the Hagley Road: 'Great naval disaster: special.' The Man, who invariably took first prep, sent out for a paper. He glanced at the paper and said: 'There has been a great naval battle in the North Sea; we have lost many ships.' He read out some of the names and I remember after night prayers hearing Goddard crying bitterly. His brother had been a midshipman in number 1 turret on the *King George V,* sunk with all hands.

All of us were going to be soldiers, with a few exceptions, like myself, who were going to try for late entry into the Navy. I slaved away at sine and cosine and the differential calculus, but I could never do even the simplest arithmetic and all the higher stuff was totally beyond me. It began to be obvious that I was never going to pass into the Royal Navy through Keyham where the essential requirement was higher mathematics.

I never knew what 'Ticky' Stark, a Cambridge wrangler, was talking about; there was an impenetrable wall between us. The future generals of the Second World War were so many Stalkies with him, liberating mice half way through his interminable two-hour periods, suddenly screaming out: 'I feel faint, sir' or, among the truly histrionic future battle commanders, staging actual faints, enabling four or five Army Class members to get out of the room at once. I took little part in any of that; I was an outcast in that company, understanding nothing, my mind elsewhere.

Happily I was more at home with Army Class history and English. There are moments when I could still draw a battle plan of Blenheim, say a little about the Battle of Borodino, talk for a minute or two about Tudor kings and for much longer about the Georges. There was the usual school murdering of Shakespeare. Because of all that, there are still plays of Shakespeare I cannot read. For much the same reason I have never been able to finish *Paradise Lost* or *The Fairy Queen.* But it does help with crosswords in later life.

Then came Armistice Day. The *Daily Chronicle* had an

arrangement of bells and ribbons across the top of every page and a banner headline: 'RING OUT THE THOUSAND YEARS OF WAR, RING IN THE THOUSAND YEARS OF PEACE.' The next time that 'thousand year' phrase was used it was by Hitler with his Thousand Year Reich.

That same term, the great 'flu epidemic of 1918, which killed more people all over the world than the war, put the whole school into bed. The Hag lay at death's door for weeks, the school boilerman died, but all the boys survived. We all went home a week early, white and thin, and with the war over. That was a dreary Christmas holiday, the first of the peace. My brother Will was back from the war, badly shattered. The country was full of men who would never be quite the same again, never be able to converse fully with people who had not been there, had not even begun to guess at the horrors of trench warfare, the dreadful consequences of politicians and generals conducting a war with all the ideas and most of the weapons of fifty years earlier. That was my last schoolboy Christmas, my last bound volume of the *BOP*. Mother decided that Christmas, that year, ought not to be 'joyful'. 'We should spend it on our knees,' she said, 'praying for mothers who have no sons home for Christmas, for afflicted persons of every kind, for grace for ourselves to endure.' I spent it shut up by myself in the dining room, my feet on the anthracite stove, reading my *BOP*.

I went back after Christmas to a different Oratory School. It was not at all bad. I had become much stronger and was able to take care of myself. Oddly enough two or three of the boys who had made my life a frightful burden of day and night misery became my closest friends. I was in the Upper School, but it never occurred to me to ask any brat to do anything for me. It was clear that I would never be able to pass into the Navy and I asked my father to get me a cadetship in the Merchant Service. My wishes completely flummoxed the Man. 'No boy from this school has ever suggested such a thing before,' he said, 'but I'll try to find out something.'

School games were now completely meaningless to me, but it was not possible to get excused from them. They built character, as everyone knew, and only the unhealthiest of boys could possibly prefer the school library. Now that I was in the Upper School I was admitted to the silent privacies of the reference library and from that moment I spent all my free time there. My last term at the Oratory was really quite happy.

A great deal of official energy went into preparation for the first camp of the postwar period, to be held at Tidworth Pennings on Salisbury Plain – which was not too bad if you didn't take it too seriously. I thought even then that the proceedings were farcical. Our OTC weapons were the kind used in South Africa against the Boers in 1900. Our commanding officer marched about with a sword. Company Sergeant Major Wharchus raved at us in language already years out of date. I entered into all of it with simulated zest. I was a lance-corporal, I knew at last how to roll a perfect puttee, how to get my boots exactly right. The Sergeant Major no longer referred to the "'ump on my back like the dome of St Paul's".

Meanwhile, I discovered English poetry in much the same way as all other schoolboys who are going to discover it at all. You are perhaps peacefully reading a chapter in some book of elementary physics about the expansion of gases. You lay it aside and open *Palgrave's Golden Treasury*. You open at random; you are tired and sleepy, and you read: 'And all night long we have not stirred, And yet God has not said a word.' And suddenly you are lost for ever.

My *Palgrave* was a shilling edition given to me by a master called Morton, who had given up a fat Anglican living to reduce himself and his wife to poverty by embracing Catholicism and being compelled to try and teach people like me. I had said something ignorant and stupid, and he had rewarded me with *Palgrave*.

Perhaps it was not Browning, perhaps not even *Palgrave*, but it was in just such a casual humdrum manner, like Beetle chancing upon 'Tom o' Bedlam' in *Curiosities of Literature*, that I took the road which led in the end to David Jones. He was then still unknown to me, but home from the wars and perhaps already forming in his mind the opening lines of *In Parenthesis*. '49 Wyatt, 0549 Wyatt. Coming, Sergeant.' Years later David Jones was to write in a preface to his 'fragments of an attempted writing', *The Anathemata*, that most of his thoughts and images came to him during Mass. Mine never came that way to me, although I tried once or twice.

David Jones of course was to come much later. But I had

taken the first step. He is difficult at first sight and perhaps you have to serve a long apprenticeship to Pound and Eliot, and above all to Joyce, to get hold of David Jones altogether. And there is something else. In *The Anathemata,* when Brendan cries out from his sea-horse: 'Mirabilis Deus in Sanctis suis', you have to believe that Brendan could quite easily, if God willed it, sail across the Atlantic on a stone slab, and discover America for the Irish long before any Norseman thought of antedating Columbus. I came to love David Jones.

There was a minor scandal in the school that term. A boy was taken away by his mother, a master left in the middle of the night, a boy went out of his mind. All very odd, most of us thought, and I never learned what happened to any of them except that one of the boys mixed up innocently in these strange events won a DSO at Alamein. When I saw this decoration gazetted I thought of that boy; I had found him in the school chapel, weeping and weeping under two tablets on the chapel wall. One of the tablets commemorated his uncle, an Oratory boy killed in the Boer War, the other his father, an Oratory boy killed in the second week of the war just over, almost the first officer casualty. His brother had just won a Victoria Cross. He wept because he had done nothing at all, nothing; and yet a master had been turned out of the school at midnight because of him. We were a strict lot, but I said I didn't think any of these things mattered. I still don't.

All that term passed in a mist. We were always parading and there was the Annual War Office Inspection. We still did everything by the *Infantry Manual,* we sloped and ported arms, we eased springs, we moved about in close or extended order, we formed fours or formed two deep. As we were all going into the Coldstream or the Grenadiers, we did Guards drill, stamping our feet, and executing an extraordinary half spring into the air as we turned about. I could still instruct a squad to fix bayonets by numbers if the need should ever arise. Come to that, I could rewrite most of the *Infantry Manual* if any museum has lost its copy.

In camp, we were brigaded with Eton and Winchester. They too still lived in the past, Eton still in their pale violet uniforms, Winchester still wearing their off-duty grey flannels with slouch hats. I was in charge of an eight-man bell tent, beginning my lifelong hatred of nights under canvas. My first duty was to carry off my little squad to the straw tent to fill palliasses. The discomfort comes back to me vividly – straw inside the shirt, the damp seeping through ground sheets, rain leaking through old tent canvas, sopping wet floor boards, daily kit inspection, the horror of latrines which, once endured, I put out of my life by walking every day to Tidworth railway station for my personal needs and regarding the mileage as well spent.

But at last camp was over, term was over, school was over. Part of my happiness in that last term had been looking forward to a holiday in Ireland which my father had arranged. And part of the pleasure was the prospect of seeing Netta.

Netta had married, as my mother had said dramatically, 'with a lie on her lips'. She had wanted a quiet wedding, but it was not to be; it was in the Lady Chapel of Westminster Cathedral and Cardinal Bourne was present. He said afterwards that he would have married her himself if he had known she was Fitz's daughter – but nobody knew that till my father stepped forward to give her away. She had pursued her old technique of pretending she didn't belong to us.

Off she had gone to Dublin with a man who despised her parents, who, in my father's favourite term, was of absolutely no account, and who died in her arms after nearly thirty years of living apart from her. No one could ever have lived *with* Netta, although scores of men would have liked to try. There can never have been a woman so lovable but so unlivable-with.

I was going first by myself to stay with Netta in Dublin and then we were all going to what my father said was an excellent hotel. But I knew better than that. I had been to one of my father's excellent hotels before. What I did not know was that in the course of the last year, quite unknown to me, my father had been taking the first steps which were to lead me into many years of frustration, disappointment, and the mismanagement of my life. He had embarked on a course which was to lead him to the brink of what he called ruin – a state much envied by numerous well-to-do people. My father might often be 'short of money', but he was never in any difficulty about getting hold of some. I recall endless rows based on my eldest sister wanting a pound or on my wanting a new suit of clothes, but I do not recall my father not having enough to buy a factory in Ealing or a row of houses. As with so many wealthy people, *his* expenditure was essential but *yours* was wasteful and probably sinful.

But so far I knew nothing of his plans. I started for Ireland simply looking forward to a holiday.

Three

I travelled to Ireland directly after camp, to stay a few days with my sister Netta. My sister lived in a vast house in Monkstown, bought for her by my father. There were three large sitting rooms which opened with folding doors to make one huge ballroom. There were long corridors leading to oak-panelled bedrooms. There was a gallery right round the entrance hall. It was, from the outside, a delightful house complete with stabling and outhouses.

When I arrived with my kitbag, the house seemed to be alive with babies and my sister pregnant with another – and in so vast a manner that she seemed like a balloon. There were several servants, one of whom shouted as I entered: 'I'll serve no soldier. No British bloodsucker shall be fed by me.' My eldest sister never changed her voice. 'Stop talking, Norah,' she said, 'and bring my brother a large breakfast on the lawn.'

I spent a happy fortnight waiting for Carrie and my parents. My sister always enjoyed causing a sensation, and I first had to be shown to her friends in my uniform. I explained that that could not be done for very long, was in fact against King's Regulations for a cadet, but I was whirled all over Dublin that first eventful day. 'This is my youngest brother, just over from his Officers' Training Corps camp.' Up would go my hand in salute. 'He's smart and handsome, don't you think,' Netta would say, 'and growing up so fast: we must find him girls.' It was an exhausting first day.

Her two little girls were as exhausting as their mother. They crawled about in what seemed to me a licentious manner; they were everywhere. There was no sign of the singular beauty which was to come to both of them. They were always dirty. The first of two little boys was still inside Netta but far from hidden and almost as pervasive as the others. 'Arrah ye shameless one' – shrieked at my sister by an old woman – was my first introduction to The Real Ireland, where it was, and still is, an occasion of sin even to *be* a woman, if not indeed a mortal sin in its own right.

By the end of my second day I knew that my sister and her husband had different ideas about everything. He was rather a neat and tidy man, a horseman, a manufacturer of horn goods, from rosary beads – a never-failing Irish market – to combs. He had herded cows in Wyoming, had been a sheriff, had hanged a man. An exciting character to meet. But what he wanted to do now was to rest at home and keep rabbits, as he had most contentedly done in the small house he had provided for my sister when he had first brought her to Ireland. He was much older than Netta and wanted now to be a home body, the very last thing in the world to make the slightest appeal to my eldest sister. She wished to be seen everywhere. She ran up enormous bills, becoming familiar with a world of duns and bailiffs, from which – as her husband could not – it became my father's almost quarterly habit to rescue her, never, alas, without acres of paper violence.

My sister could write letters which burned holes in ordinary writing paper and would have inflicted damage on asbestos. My father carried these wounding documents about with him, reading them over and over again – but my sister had forgotten what was in her letters as she dropped them into the post box. It was impossible to get this into my father's head. And every time she wrote Netta wanted money, and wanted it badly. The actual extraction of it had to be done by my mother who could do anything she wished with my father.

So when Netta wrote to my father for money – putting into her letter some general observations about his lifelong meanness and his obvious hatred of her, shown by penny-pinching her in her poverty-stricken married state after bringing her up to be rich and important – when she added that death would be welcome, that a convent would at last bring peace to her tortured soul, that she loved her children – *his* grandchildren – even as they wasted away from the starvation imposed upon them by him, her own father – though not so much a father as a monster, one who had ruined not only her life but the lives of her mother, her brothers and sisters and most of the people surrounding him – when this had been written and posted and Netta had gone back singing to the house bought by my father to make her

62

happy in faraway Dublin – it was my mother who was faced with the double task of comforting my grief-stricken father and getting him to write out a cheque for several hundred pounds.

I could see on my first visit to Montpelier Manor that a period of crisis was at hand. My sister's husband was out a lot at night, playing poker; he never seemed to get any breakfast; there was a lot of chaos and not enough furniture.

I inspected the hotel in Kingstown where we were all to stay. It was not, as Netta hoped, the rather grand Royal Pier Hotel but a sort of boarding house annexe which I most certainly *had* expected. Will had been earning his own money since long before the war, Tom was a priest and independent of my father, Carrie was a daughter of the house, living at home, Netta was married, I was a schoolboy. We were all to stay in this dismal annexe. I never had any money except the postal orders sent to me at school by Mother, or the half crowns she slipped into my hand in the holidays. My father had a simple answer to any request for money I might nerve myself to make. 'If I give you any money, you will spend it.' He never thought of himself as *spending* money, only as using it. It was people like his spendthrift youngest son who spent money and brought everyone to ruin. *He* was not going to waste money on grand hotels for a family holiday.

The first crisis came with the arrival of the mailboat holding Mother, my father, and Carrie. I stood on the pier at Kingstown, and there they were waving at me as the ship tied up. As we walked along the pier, Mother said: 'Does Cissie like her piano?' She always called Netta Cissie, and Cissie always hated it. 'What piano?' I said, 'there isn't one in the Manor.' Mother stood quite still for a moment with her hand over her heart. 'Oh my God,' she said at last, 'not a word to your father, dear, not a word, until I have seen Cissie and then spoken to him.'

That was the beginning of a holiday which had every ingredient of Russian tragedy. That holiday involved huge sums of money, twenty years of debt, my next forty years, Carrie's whole life, fantastic changes for Mother, nightmares of difficulty, misunderstanding, and endless situations which make *The Cherry Orchard* and *Uncle Vanya* seem uproarious comedies. Houses were built in absurd places as a result of that holiday, unsuitable marriages took place, private chapels were constructed, Carrie was ejected from convents, even a dog, at that moment peacefully in Radlett, had years later to be shot because of that holiday.

Netta's missing piano set the tone from the start. She had begged for a piano, my mother had pleaded with my father to buy one for her and at last he had yielded and arranged for a rosewood baby grand to be shipped to Ireland. It had arrived at a bad moment; Netta was being dunned by a large drapery firm and she sold the piano to pay her debts. No one ever knew what passed between my mother and father, but no one ever heard the matter referred to again.

Netta having already got two babies was not too strongly in the limelight with the new one. I was the one in the limelight. There was to be a career for me and I was to be a farmer. This had been discussed in an atmosphere of complete unreality from time to time after my father had talked over my merchant service aspirations with a number of his grand shipping friends. It seemed that his friend in Cunard – I never heard his name – said that they liked their cadets out of training ships and much younger than me. The friend had said, also, that he couldn't see much of a career in it for 'Fitz's boy'. There was another friend in the Grace Line who apparently owned it. He thought that any son of Fitz's would be a little out of place. There were others, and they all seemed to have made a great deal of money through not going to sea; they all advised people like my father to keep their children on dry land.

Finally my father made up his mind: 'Promotion in the Merchant Service,' he announced one night in his pontifical way, 'is a matter of Freemasonry; and there is no chance of reaching the Board from the Deck.' He always spoke in capital letters like that, pausing to emphasise each word, weighing one sentence against another, achieving a verbal balance which fascinated all of us. It was characteristic that he was thinking of my place on the board of a shipping line while my mind was running on a junior cadetship. I was to be a disappointment in that way to a great many people as my life went along. I never thought much of boards, or of most of the people who strove to be on them.

I had the illusion, common to a great many schoolboys, that life in an office would kill me. The Bar was discussed, my father pointing out that this would involve the great expense of university education. I think he always thought of university people as men talking about Latin – perhaps actually *in* Latin – while living a life of sin. He could himself talk any don into the ground, had read immensely over a wide field and had a really serious mind. He had spent the whole of his first week's wages, the first money he had ever earned, on a copy of Byron's poems – a battered little book with a brown paper cover. He could see no point in others taking a more expensive path to a goal he had reached through pleasure in what he called The Things of the Mind. 'Cultivate an Orderly Mind, my Son,' he would say, 'Dwell on the Things of the Mind, Live in Them.' There was nothing of the Podsnap or Pecksniff about my father as he said these things. He believed in them, lived them himself. Never once in all his life did I know him to impute an unworthy motive behind the words and actions of anyone.

The idea of the Bar was abandoned and the idea of 'farming' became more and more to the forefront of our talks. I had enjoyed my wartime voluntary stints with Farmer Smith of Radlett, I began to see myself striding across fields, thinking about cutting 'that meadow hay', 'the farm' a nebulous, buttercuppy place.

A week after the arrival of my parents, my father said he was going down into Tipperary and would take me with him. We were to stay in a place called Thurles, which it seemed everyone called Thur-less. The train journey from Dublin to Thurles was the dreariest I ever remember, through some of the saddest-looking country in the world. It made me miserable then, and it does still. All the railways of Ireland were built to strategic plans, and to aid troop movements, not to serve the populace. Not that by the time the railways were being built there was much of a populace to serve; they had crossed the Atlantic, driven out of Ireland by the great hunger.

We drove from the station at Thurles in a vehicle unknown in England at any time, an 'inside car'. Perhaps its nearest equivalent was the early-nineteenth-century French or Swiss 'diligence', uncomfortable seats placed lengthwise, the floor deep in straw. Ireland at that time was still full of outside cars, what the English called 'jaunting cars'. They have gone forever, but if you knew how to sit on one, and were not afraid, they were very comfortable.

Our inside car took us to the Munster Hotel, a dreary enough spot opposite the obviously principal hotel in the place, Hayes's. I asked my father why we were staying in such a dump, with a decent-looking spot across the road. 'Because, my son, I have stayed here, each time I have come to Thurles, for over thirty years.' It was then that I began to discover why everyone knew my father and to find out about the major part he had played in the establishment of the Creamery Movement, the forgotten foundation stone of the present Republic. There could never have been a free Ireland without the possibility of a self-supporting Ireland. The Creamery Movement of Plunkett* and AE was the first rushlight in the dark of total dependence on England. Those two, Plunkett and AE, preached the gospel of a Co-operative Marketing Movement for the dairy products of the small farmer, which would enable him to get his head above water. But it would have come to nothing if my father had not guaranteed a market for every box of butter that would come out of an Irish creamery. He never went back on that.

There was a fête in Thurles that night and my father and I went to it. Irish 'fairs', a thing of the past now, were strictly for the buying and selling of livestock. The fêtes were much like those in England, except for their emphasis on physical pro-wess. There was a 'skyrider' installed at the fête in Thurles and my father asked me if I thought I was strong enough to risk it. I thought I was. You climbed to the top of a tower from which a wire was stretched to the ground a hundred or so yards away. You held on to a wheeled bar and stepped off the tower. If you were not strong enough you let go and were seriously hurt. I proved strong enough but glad to reach the grass.

It was late when we got back to the Munster Hotel. My father suggested a wash and we walked together to the only bathroom. I hit my head severely passing through the low door. We washed and I struck my head against the lintel as we went out. My father said: 'That is very interesting, my son. Thirty years ago I struck my head coming into this bathroom and I have never done it since. You have done it twice in less than five minutes. That augurs ill for your future life.' It did indeed.

Our meal was a mish-mash of mutton, strong black tea,

*Sir Horace Plunkett, 1854-1932.

barnbrack – a sort of cake-bread – soda bread, and wedges of butter, which reminded me of why the founder of the Birmingham Oratory had never succeeded in his plan for a Catholic University in Ireland. As if a man like Newman could ever have succeeded in a country like Ireland! He was a delicate fastidious man, all scholar and aesthete, a master stylist, a man with more than half his mind in heaven. He had said of the Irish clergy: 'They seem to live on raw and bleeding mutton, and their hands are dirty.' That finished Newman in Ireland; that and the dreadful Cardinal Primate of the time who loathed people like him. I thought of all that, as I ate my raw and bleeding mutton and sipped at the black tea. I was very much a Newman man and I still am. I sometimes even suspect myself of being very much an Oratory boy.

After supper we sat, amidst straw, talking to people about everything under the sun. Farmers they all were, typical Irish small farmers, the salt of the country. We talked of everything but at the back of everyone's mind lay the question: 'What do they want?'

They knew my father; perhaps he was down on some creamery business. But what was this boy doing? The tension grew and grew and at last a man whose name I never learned blurted it out. 'Mr FitzGerald,' he said, 'is it true that you have bought Synone?' 'Yes,' my father said, 'it is true; I have bought Synone.'

While they gaped at him my mind rushed back to Radlett and my father producing a map. 'He must be going to buy some land in Ireland,' Will had said, 'but he can't be going to buy a place like that. It's big enough to have villages on it.' Well, it was big for Ireland, 986 acres, and he had bought it. I was to go there tomorrow. 'I have bought it for my Benjamin here,' my father said.

Early next morning we made a start in an old Ford taxi, the Model T Ford which no one under the age of sixty-five can remember, the car you played like an organ with your feet if all was going well and with your fingers on a set of shock-administering tremblers if they were not. This was the car you got into shape for starting with kettles of boiling water poured over the exhaust manifold, or with one of the back wheels jacked off the ground – the car which repaid you for these ministrations by either breaking your wrist in frightening back-spins from the starting handle or by dashing forward off its chocks and pinning you against the nearest wall.

We came to Synone. There was a broken down lodge gate, a broken down pair of cottages serving as lodge, three-quarters of a mile of avenue and then the house. It was a hideous house, built in 1860 under a grant from the Board of Works. The walls were two feet thick and made of weeping limestone; there were two staircases, a complex of pantries and still-rooms, an enormous kitchen built over cool dairies, a wine cellar and a laundry. The house had nothing to do with the country in which it stood. It was an English farm house, built for English farming, in those English counties where farms were big. There were only six bedrooms but four of them were very large. It was obvious as we came into the house that the real life of the place was in a back office-like room; that the occupants hardly ever used the principal living rooms and that all the chimneys smoked. My heart sank a little but my father was tremendously elated. Here he was 'where he wished to be', on his own acres in Ireland. For the first of many hundred times he spoke the words he was to use for the rest of his life every time he looked across the forty-acre Lawn Field. 'This is a lovely, lovely place.' I never thought that.

We drove all over the entire farm in a trap behind 'Brownie', the cob who was still alive with us, and still going strong, fifteen years later. The yards and stock buildings were almost a hamlet on their own. There was Jack Heffernan's cottage; he was the working steward. There was Miss Wilson's cottage; she was a friend of the Nicolson family. There was a wonderful piece of surviving horsegear operating machinery – a power unit driven by horses that could be used for thrashing or anything else. There were acres of barn. There were tie stalls for fattening fifty heifers and three open yards for fattening bullocks. There was a blacksmith's forge, two vast machine storage sheds, five stable buildings, half a dozen loose boxes, a harness room. There were seventeen tied cottages on the place and twenty-three men employed. All this would say to me later, when I knew more: 'This is good second-class land which will need a great deal of sheer farming to keep it up.'

It was an exciting day. When we left, there was a plan for me to return in October and to work on the place until Christmas. That was something to look forward to.

That evening I heard that for the first time in his life my father had gone directly against my mother's wishes and had also broken a promise he had made to her. He had set off from England weeks before to look at Synone. He had promised faithfully not to do anything final until he had returned and talked it over with Mother. He had come back with Synone in his pocket and apparently Mother had uttered words which I was never to forget: 'No luck will come to any of us with that place.' And no luck ever did.

My father salved his conscience by insisting that he had bought Synone for me. Of course he had bought Synone for himself and demonstrated that from the first day. But his luck was running out. He had not paid for Synone. The money was not to become due for a year, nor were we to move in before Michaelmas. My father put the purchase money, about thirty thousand pounds in those distant times, into French rents with the Credit Lyonnais. He knew with certainty that Monsieur Clemenceau meant what he said, that the French franc would never, ever, be devalued. The French franc was devalued almost as soon as my father's money was in Lyons. He was to be in debt to one bank or another for the next twenty years.

What a holiday that was! Practically everything that could go wrong went wrong. I remember a happy day in the Wicklow Hills. In Radlett my father had had a friend who was the top salesman in England for an American firm, the National Cash Register Company. There were two staggeringly beautiful daughters and two sons who went to school in France. Suddenly some mysterious piece of bad luck descended on the father and the whole family vanished to Ireland. I suppose the father took to drink, or put a hand in the till, or committed some crime against American business, like taking half a day off one month, or not selling twice as much as he had sold the year before. Whatever it was, they vanished overnight, reappearing in a small country house in the South of Ireland. And down to Wicklow I went to see them.

I remember being met by the second son, in the highest high trap I had ever seen; we were yards off the ground and it was put to a good-going horse, a trotter of about sixteen hands. We had a good day at their comfortable house and I returned to our Kingstown hotel full of what I had seen and of their kindness, bursting to tell all. And there, behind my father, shaking her head, putting fingers to her lips, as she had so often to do all her life, was my mother.

There must have been some discussion between them while I was away; perhaps there had been a storm and my mother did not want to start it again. I only gradually learnt that in fact my father had paid for the horse, the high trap, my pleasant entertainment and a good deal more. He thought he was sending an old friend the money to pay an urgent debt, a thing he never ceased to do with any old friend all his life. The debt was never paid, the money was always spent, my father never saw it again. It's a useful technique, if you can learn it.

That was the year of the first big postwar strike, and there was no boat home and no trains were running in England. I can still feel my father's irritation. He needed to be back in England, and therefore this strike was against *him* personally. Needless to say we were on the very first totally overcrowded boat and the first totally overcrowded train from Holyhead. My father pressed an enormous tip, one shilling, into the hand of a ticket inspector at Holyhead and asked him to 'keep us all together'. That is just what he did, revenging himself nicely by pushing me, my mother, Carrie and my father into a third-class compartment, the door of which he locked, and which had no proper lighting, the gas flickering just outside the mantle, creating blue shadows. My father fell instantly and peacefully asleep; my mother, Carrie and I stayed awake through the long night to Euston. We were glad to get to Radlett and Desmond Cottage. I was still cluttered with kitbags, uniforms, school clothes. But I was finished with all that. I was home for good; I had left school.

A month later I was back in Ireland and at Synone in nice time for the turnip snagging. There were early frosts that year and they soon claimed me as a victim. Snagging turnips was done with a heavy, extremely sharp, chopping knife. The back is bent, the ice-covered leaves grasped, the root pulled clear. The taper on the root is first chipped off and the turnip held out by its bunch of leaves, the chopper being brought down smartly across the neck. If all this is done correctly the leafless turnip should fall neatly between the rows of plants, the leaves being dropped at the feet. Sheep will safely graze them later on. The back should not be straightened between turnips or the operator will quite soon be unable to bear the agony of bending, straightening, and re-bending. The row stretches ahead of you for miles – or so it seems. At each end, it is permissible to stand erect for a moment before resuming. In theory, you chat happily to your companions on either side as the little snagging team moves slowly up and down the turnip field. Four rows are snagged into one to make carting off easier.

But suppose all this is not done correctly? Then, the bunches of icy leaves will freeze the unaccustomed soft hand. Both hands will be affected, the knife hand more slowly but just as surely. Disaster waits. In my case, it came soon. A large turnip confronted me and I pulled it clear. I shook off the loose dirt, trimmed the 'taper' and struck at the neck with my numbed hand. Across my left thumb now lies a deep scar, there for life. I got it on my first turnip row, on my first morning as a farm labourer at Synone. There were four of us, and my wound made a nice break for my companions. They were happy to wait, standing upright, while I got a handkerchief round my thumb. Then we went on. I knew I had to do that. I was the new owner's son and under close observation, probably from everyone for miles around, most certainly from every employee.

That was at eight o'clock in the morning, and the dinner break of an hour and a half began at twelve. There were four more hours to go, and it soon became clear that my back would not last four hours. But I must make it. Every now and then my kind companions reached across to my rows and 'did a few'. Those were blessed, blessed, gaps to reach. Suddenly there was a lovely bare stretch and you were up with the others again. Just before the farm bell tolled in the great yard to say that it was twelve o'clock and we were free until half past one, I sliced through my index finger. Then I walked back to the house for my dinner. I thought I had done a good morning's work. I did not dream that the afternoon was to be worse.

In the house they laughed at my two bound up fingers, and gave me plaster for them. I ate a great deal and, keen young

71

tyro, was out in the yard as the bell was tolled. It tolled for me. We were, I learned, to thrash rakings.

In those days of tied sheaves and huge ricks in beautifully kept rickyards – 'haggards' in Ireland – there was always one large rick of rubbish that was eventually thrashed out for poultry or animals. It was made from the rakings of all the harvest fields. After the sheaves had been gathered in, the horse rakes went up and down the corn fields gathering the stray cornstalks into rows. These were forked on to carts and brought home to sheds, Dutch barns, or put together in any way which was not too much trouble. About a quarter of the stuff was sound corn, the rest weeds, weed seeds, and the dust and dirt picked up by the rakes. Thrashing that lot out was always and anywhere a dirty filthy job, and the dirtiest, filthiest task was that of standing on the thrashing mill with a fork and steering the great pitching forksful of tangled rubbish, as it was flung down on to the thrashing platform, towards the 'feeder' man who stood in a kind of metal trench immediately behind and above the spinning thrashing drum. They gave the job to me.

There was no rest of any kind. The old creamery steam engine puffed and roared away, the mass of belts and wheels which made up those old thrashing machines spun and turned, the dust rose in clouds, filling every nostril, and choking the unaccustomed me. It did not seem possible that I could last out until six, the official finishing hour; it wouldn't matter at that sort of work if it grew a bit dark towards that hour at that time of year. There was no need to take care with rakings, no fear of sticking a fork into the feed man, or of the binder twine knives slipping in the wrong direction and cutting a throat. No one seemed in the least tired, no one seemed to want a drink, or to knock off for what were called in those days 'natural functions'. But God was on the side of His smallest and least important battalion; He sent some rain. That wouldn't have mattered for the rakings, but there was enough of it to make the main driving belt slippery. After it had flown off three times, Jack Heffernan called off the operation and I was free to get into the house. I had a luke warm bath, an enormous tea and went to bed. I had to be up at six next morning.

I spent the whole of my second day in that turnip field. Shea's Field was nearly fifty acres between hedges and fences and each

72

dead straight turnip row was a good four hundred yards. It seemed longer. I was to get to know that area better, but on that second day I did not know very much about anything. By the six o'clock bell, I was a deaf, dumb, blind, exhausted old man.

My third morning at Synone was fine and dark, but my left hand had stiffened up with its two savage cuts on the backs of thumb and forefinger and I went across to the yard at the seven o'clock bell dreading the unending ordeal of the turnip field. But it was to be three years before I snagged another root, and that was a long way from Tipperary.

Jack Heffernan conducted every open-air conversation in a voice which Stentor would have considered excessive. He began roaring out the day's orders before any of the men in question were more than gloomy shadows in autumnal mists. 'Good morning, Master Kevin,' he shouted, 'you're going ploughing this morning with Michael Barratt.' Those words prefaced the happiest day of my life.

A great many people have written a great deal on the subject of ploughing with a pair of horses. Soon there won't be anyone left to add another first-hand account. There has never been a more beautiful outdoor activity. There has never been a bad-tempered ploughman. His whole life style leads to a calm appreciation of existence, a placid acceptance of a happy lot, a relationship with a pair of horses so close as to suggest the harmony of a ballerina with her partner, rather than an ordinary day's work on an ordinary farm.

Everything that morning was strictly as it should be. No part of the ritual was omitted. The horses were 'in' for the hard work of the winter, although there would still be a few weekends when they would have a Saturday night and the whole of Sunday in the fields. Michael Barratt took me into his stable and introduced me to his team. He was to be 'Mick' within the hour, and 'Mick' as I sat holding his hand by his death bed thirty years later, my whole life changed, his precisely the same. My father had still to learn that those horses, and Jim Ryan's horses, and Mike Ryan's horses, were not really his, but theirs; he paid for them, fed them, housed them, paid for their replacement – but in no sense owned them. They knew to whom they belonged, whose voice to acknowledge, at whom to look round as the baskets of oats were carried each night into their stables. They did not give my father the wonderful snuffled greeting of the horse as he peered into their stables and boxes in after years; that was for Mick and the Ryans, for Jimmy Lawrence, Patsy Heffernan, Mickie Murphy and the other horsemen. Now and again it would be for me.

That was the morning I discovered that horses loved ploughing, loved being out for the day free from shafts. They knew what was going to happen as they turned their heads to thrust into the collar and hames and felt the back strap and chains go on, instead of the high padded straddle for shaft work. All that was the prelude to the first of the classic moments of a ploughing day, the setting off of the ploughman, sitting sideways on his land horse, his furrow horse on a lead rope, to the spot where yesterday's stint had finished.

The horse plough in use all over Ireland at that time was the Ransome IRDCP 3 – how easily those initials and the number flash into the mind and on to the page after more than half a century! It was a steep-breasted digger plough, with a short strongly curved mouldboard to break the furrow as it was laid by the plough, and a soft iron plough point, renewed every few acres.

The plough is a symbol throughout the world of peace and fertility, an ideal object into which warriors have eventually to beat their swords. As I suppose the first sight of any great and simple thing must always be, my first sight of my first plough was something of a disappointment. A plough at rest, stuck overnight into the beginning of a new furrow, is merely a rusty-looking piece of farm equipment, the silvery bright share and mouldboard buried in the ground. At that stage a plough reveals nothing of itself other than its total inviolability. This has to be learnt by word of mouth, casually, and perhaps many days later. No man would dream of stealing or interfering with a plough. The IRDCP 3 which Mick and I reached that morning before eight o'clock had only lain there since the previous night. It could well have been there for twenty years. No one would have laid hands on it.

A horse plough looks simple but in fact is very complicated. Lying beside it, linked by chains, are three pieces of timber, the swingletrees. The main piece, to which the other two are linked, has a central hook. That is to hitch the whole contraption to the plough. The swingletrees govern the depth of the furrow and they are hooked to the plough at any of six or eight indentations at the head of the main plough beam. A ploughman may not be able to read much more than the important bits of the local paper, or to write much more than his name. But he has at his fingertips a working knowledge of mechanical engineering. The swingletrees are only the first and easiest part of getting the right depth of furrow, of 'setting the plough'.

It is not difficult to hitch a pair of horse by chains to a set of swingletrees, but you have to be shown how to do it a good deal oftener than once, and you must learn not to be frightened about getting mixed up with the hind legs of horses and pushing them about a little to make the work easier and simpler. And you must join the horses together, with crossed ropes at their heads, so that they move in unison at a touch on the plough lines, long lengths of rope, looped at the ends for convenience in holding, or hanging on the plough handles if the horses are resting. I have heard of fancy ploughmen with leather lines and partially leather-covered chains, and once or twice I have seen them at competitions, though I never knew a judge influenced by gear unless a particular class in the competition was for 'done up' horses in full trappings. But I was learning to plough for workaday farming and all the equipment was working tackle. All the same, Mick Barratt was champion ploughman of Tipperary, the title won in full open competition, although never acknowledged for one moment by Jim Ryan, who had come second, having slightly cut his furrow horse while trimming its tail with a pocket knife, which made it a little jumpy on the morning of the great day.

'I got a pound and a sack of flour,' Mick said, 'a fine sum of money and a great prize altogether.' His wages when he began to teach me to plough were the grazing of an ass, the free ploughing and preparation of a quarter of an Irish acre* of potato ground – for which he was docked eightpence a week – and seventeen and sixpence every Friday night. These were high wages for those days immediately after the First World War, and he got free straw for his pig too. He paid a shilling a week for his cottage, one of the beautiful thatched Irish cottages of the Paul

*An Irish acre was 1¼ English acres.

Henry pictures, riddled with dirt and tuberculosis, utterly lacking in any privacy for the rearing of a family, the nearest water maybe a mile or half a mile away, every activity of the human body exposed to view, or carried out at night or in secret. Thank God they are all gone now.

It has been said that the finest cure for almost every kind of mental distress – from a hangover to matrimonial disaster – is a day with a pair of horses and a plough. That remedy is now denied to all in the so-called developed countries. The poor in undeveloped lands have it still. But perhaps, since they have never been deprived of the plough, they don't feel the need for the remedy.

The horses move forward along your first furrow. You begin murmuring to them. 'Hub orf,' you say, or 'Hub in,' and they respond, gently altering the line of tug, approaching or slightly moving away from each other, taking part in the work, enjoying it. If a tractor-pulled plough hits a buried rock either the wooden safety plug on the hitching apparatus gives or parts of the machinery will twist out of true or break. With a pair of horses, as the plough point touches the unyielding buried object, they stop. You pull the plough back, take the narrow spade from its rack along the handles, dig out the boulder, throw it on to the ploughed land, and go ahead. A well-trained pair of horses and a well-set plough require very little attention on the way to the headland – the end of the row. Machines need a fifteen-yard headland in which to turn, a horse plough five. And the turning is the high point of skill in the whole operation. Ragged edges and a cut-up headland are the marks of the novice. At the exact moment when the plough point reaches the end of the furrow the plough must be jerked out of the ground with the hip-twist lying at the heart of the mystery.

As that happens the horses will begin to turn sharply in, and they must be protected from themselves, or the land horse will tread on the feet of the furrow horse, taking off a shoe, or worse. This is almost the only moment, recurring at each end of the field at the end of each furrow, when it may be necessary to have a light hand on the plough lines. 'Keep off,' you say, 'keep off,' and as delicately as a fly fisherman you touch the offside ploughline. At once the land horse moves out a little, and avoids his partner's feet.

76

That is all; that is all you have to do. Behind you, coming from nowhere, a long line of rooks, seagulls, sometimes starlings will swarm along the new furrow. Like a robin beside a gardener's spade, they are looking for worms, grubs, wireworms. The rook, so often revengefully shot at harvest time, or on the nests of spring, is the genuine friend of all farmers. Rooks eat leatherjackets, cockchafer grubs, all sorts of earthbound vermin. Nor do they beat down corn as pigeons will. And a rookery brings luck. Rooks go away from places and houses which are doomed. They like happy places, with a happy family nearby.

All that and much more Mick told me on that first day, walking tirelessly beside me on the unploughed land, talking to his horses, talking to me. And as dusk fell he took the lines from me. 'There is a little thing to be done, Master Kevin,' he said 'look along the furrow now.' Alas, there was a perceptible curve beginning to show in the work, and the essence of good horse ploughing is perfect symmetry. A furrow should be the shortest distance between the two headlands, perfectly straight like a line out of Euclid. 'Wait here now,' Mick said, and off he went with his team on a round of our 'back'. He straightened the work. That is the touch of the master ploughman, to iron out the mistakes of his pupil, to leave for the night the whole 'stetch' as he has begun it in the morning. As Mick came back to me down the return furrow, running the plough effortlessly along the headland, ignoring the deep slashes I had made during the day as the plough slipped off my hip, or a clutch at a handle had dug it into the ground, he stopped and said: 'Go round this time by yourself, there's a reason.'

It was growing dark as I set off and it was nearly black dark as I came down the long beautifully easy straight furrow that Mick had prepared for me. The headland as I reached it was full of dark shadows – the rest of the men going home, most of them a bit out of their way, all of them intent on seeing the son of the new owner shaping to the work which was the foundation of all their lives. The moment is in my mind for ever, a part of my life. I can remember praying: 'Let me make the turn; let me make the turn' – and then I was jerking out the plough, the horses were turning in, the plough running smoothly along the headland to the end of the 'stetch', the furrow horse coming in perfectly, the plough dropping into the land, the horses stopping, their day's work at an end. 'That was nice, Master Kevin,' said Jim Ryan, speaking for them all.

The men went on home, Mick and I unhitched the team and got up sideways into our homegoing positions. It was black dark when we reached the yard, hung up the ploughing gear on the great wooden pegs behind each stall, rubbed down the horses with wisps of straw, fed them, and were finished for the day. I said goodnight to Mick, gave the stable lantern to Jack Heffernan at his cottage door in the yard, and walked over to the house for my tea and bed.

Yes, I suppose that was the happiest day of my life. There were to be some good days in the years ahead, but they were different. Perhaps a day in the mountains is as good, but I never found anything to beat the pleasure of ploughing with a pair of horses, on a fine October day in a vanished Ireland.

The onset of winter on a big farm like Synone means a time of endless and strenuous work. And the late autumn and early winter of 1919 marked both a high point in old-style Irish village farming and the collapse of a political system. In early November of that year barley reached a price that was then a record – 60 shillings per barrel of fourteen stones – and Inspector Hayes of the Royal Irish Constabulary was shot dead at the Fair of Thurles.* One event marked the end of a part of Irish agricultural history, the other a terrible bloodstained beginning. Both affected thousands and thousands of lives – and among them mine.

That autumn, before my father had completed his purchase, when Synone and all its takings were still Mrs Nicolson's, there was nothing you couldn't sell off a farm. And Mrs Nicolson fairly and honourably took every advantage of that situation. The 'haggard', the English rickyard, was a wonderful sight when we began the serious business of full-scale thrashing. There were, I remember, fourteen great stacks of barley, all neatly thatched, a dozen of oats, two of wheat. Under trees by the yard the potato pits were being got ready, and the endless

*In Ireland, but never in England, grain was measured by the 'barrel', though never put into an actual barrel.

labour of mucking out the open bullock-fattening yards was in full swing.

Synone was farmed on what was called an extended four course. That meant that after the barley, undersown with grass seeds, the resulting meadows were left down to grass for at least three and sometimes four years. It also meant, on a place as big as Synone, that some two hundred acres of land had to be broken every year, and of that, all the land destined for root crops had to be given huge quantities of farmyard manure. To provide that scores of bullocks – their horns brutally removed – were penned in open yards sheltered at one end, scores of heifers were tied up in long byres, and all winter long a man, a horse and a cart did nothing all day but put straw under these beasts, every day of the week. In the yards, as the winter went by, the bullocks, treading their straw, rose steadily above ground level. From the byres the dung was carted out to great dung heaps, which also received the wastages from the cow shed. It was all prodigal in the extreme of labour, then the cheapest item on the farm, now of course the dearest.

Dunging out the yards was as usual appallingly hard work for me. Every horse and cart on the place was employed, strung out between the yards and the field to be dunged. Sometimes this was a mile away, sometimes almost to hand. That autumn the main field was to hand, and that meant scarcely any interval between the departure of a full cart and the arrival of another to gather a fresh load. It meant no rest for me.

The method of getting out the dung was simple enough on paper, as are all farm activities. With one of the great two-handled hay knives, used for cutting hay, compressed by time and weight, out of the long ricks made in early summer, deep incisions were made in the four- to five-feet-thick densely pack-ed manure. Then in theory, layer by gentle layer, the dung was lifted out by four-pronged long-handled forks, and heaved into the carts. But those were the days of long straw. Wheat straw was five feet long and could be more, a wonderful waving sight when growing, a ferocious handicap when forking out. Barley straw was also much longer than it is now. Oat straw is edible and never used under cattle.

The unskilled forker (me) found himself struggling to pitch a forkful of manure into the cart, only to find that he was standing on one end of his burden. After a few hours of this, large blisters would appear between thumb and forefinger of both hands. But the house was mercifully near and as the blisters burst they could be covered with bits of plaster. I still have the marks of those. When I entered Canada as an immigrant the doctor at Quebec said: 'What makes you think you could do agricultural work with those pretty lily-white hands?' I held them out to him 'Yeah,' he said, 'what a surprise; you done it.' I had indeed.

On my first day in the dung yards there was a dreadful complication. All the men smoked plug tobacco in covered pipes, clays or cheap briers with serrated 'safety' metal tops, rather like the bottle tops of today. I smoked a pipe regularly by then and I thought I would like to try a pipeful of plug. It was Paddy Ryan Peake who prepared my downfall, cutting a piece from his plug, rubbing it down, holding out his palm with the fill. Oh Lord. That was sixty years ago and again the waves of nausea are sweeping over me. Without warning I brought up my heart. Paddy Ryan Peake covered my breakfast and what I felt was much of my inside with the forkful of manure he was about to lift into the waiting cart. Then he dug his fork in again, and pitched the lot towards next year's turnips. 'Sometimes, Master Kevin,' he said, ''tis very hard to follow the will of God.'

By the time we opened the first rick of barley for threshing, my hands were a text book of infirmity, but they were hardening, would soon not mind what they did. Opening ricks was tricky but enjoyable and I was unaware, until I read Colin Kirkus's *Come Climbing* many years later, that I was receiving a useful early lesson in what was to become a major passion in my life. The long, long, farm ladders of those days were laid flat against the slopes of the rick, so that the climb to the summit began at least ten or twelve feet out. You stepped off the ladder on to the pinnacle, the roof truss of the stack, and gingerly, balancing on nothing twenty-five feet up, began peeling off the thin protective thatch with an ordinary two-pronged harvest fork. This is a dangerous implement if you fall; you must learn to throw it away in the moment of crisis. I learnt that in a hard school, falling off moving carts when carting out turnips or fodder to outlying cattle and sheep, falling off cutting-out platforms on hayricks, but fortunately not falling off barley stacks. That would have meant serious injury.

All thrashing was exhausting work. Carrying two-hun-dredweight sacks of grain, first to a cart, and from it in due course up perhaps two sets of loft ladders to a clean grain floor – that needed the cream of the younger general labourers. A man had to be found – with us it was Jim Ryan Furry Corner – who knew enough about threshing machines to walk round and round all day with an oiler, to find time to rake up the chaff which fell through the shakers into an always growing pile, to hold up the work for the absolute minimum of time if a minor belt needed rejoining or other repair. All the work needed super-vision by Jack Heffernan, his voice rising above the humming booming noise of the thresher and engine as he shouted for more steam pressure, a quicker feed from the stack, a better clearance of chaff, and a smoother exchange of men. There were men coming and going all the time; there were short-time helpers from cow byres, pig pens, sick animals; there were men being sent away from the thrashing to help in some animal crisis reported by one of the two shepherds from some remote part of the farm. But there was no respite for me.

To the difficulty of standing on long straw, which I had met in the manure yards, was now added the danger of standing high on the thin ridge of a corn stack trying to fork out a sheaf of barley the end of which was lapped under the one carrying your feet. That kind of foolishness could put you straight over the side of the rick. I was saved twice in the first couple of hours. After that I began to learn. Those old farm activities were like huge-scale games of spillikins. Everything came away easily if you took care that nothing else was touching it.

David Jones had not then written *In Parenthesis*. Much of it would have comforted me in those days of endless physical labour. 'The thudding and breath to breath, you don't know which way, what way,' was written about soldiers in difficulty but applies to all exertion which is beyond one's powers but which still has to be kept up at full stretch. There was no dust and dirt here, to fill the throat and nostrils with filth, as in the thrashing of rakings. There was only the endless – the utterly endless – forking out to the feeder. And the work grew harder as the day advanced. At first you would be throwing down the sheaves on to the drum platform. As the day went on, you would find yourself level with it; all too soon you would have to begin pitching up. I was to know harder, longer, physical labours in the years ahead, but I was by then better prepared. At this stage, I was a farm labourer out of a drawing room.

As the rick sank we turned up an occasional mouse nest, beating out the tiny lives with our forks, but we knew that, all the time, underneath us there would be retreating rats. A foot or two above ground, darkness coming on, the job nearly done, the rats would begin to break cover. By that time sundry idlers from round about would have strayed into the haggard with their mongrel terriers. I never saw a rat get away. Of course if a weasel – there are no true weasels in Ireland; they are all the somewhat larger stoats, but the name holds – if a weasel has made his home in a corn stack there will be no rats, mice or other small deer. In a corn stack the weasel was very much the farmer's friend.

At the end of the day I had a meat tea – soda bread, barnbrack, eggs and bacon, cold ham, jam tarts or fruit pies – and went to bed. On Sundays I walked down the long Mass path across many of our fields and attended Mass in the chapel in Boherlahan. These paths honeycombed the place, as did the public house and meeting-place footpaths surviving in England. The chapel was no place for a son of Cardinal Newman from the Oratory School. I have seen some dreadful examples of Irish Catholic tastelessness since; the cathedral in Thurles takes some beating, as does the Catholic church in Cashel, but I did not know then the extent of the horror.

There were three galleries in the chapel, and they represented the class structure of the parish. The common herd, which included me – son of a father who believed he fought a life-long battle for a classless society – crowded in to the cheap pitch-pine benches in the body of the chapel. The two wing galleries on the two sides of the sanctuary held the pick of the small farmers; beneath them were the more religiously minded of the whole parish – men one side, women the other. Their frequent ecstatic groanings seriously interrupted every service.

At the back of the chapel was yet another gallery. Here sat the young blood of the parish, the up-and-coming youth, those who had been as far as Dublin, those who were training to be doctors or vets or engineers. Later I found it held some delightful and irresponsible girls. I joined them, but not that year. Many of the congregation never entered the chapel at all but knelt in a confused muddle on the gravel outside. I never got to the bottom of who came in and who stayed out.

Catholic chapels had once been prohibited. It was Cardinal Curran who built them all over Ireland in the late seventies and early eighties of last century, and thereby set up the Sunday-suit bourgeoisie from which Ireland has not yet begun to recover. Christianity, but only in Ireland, has proved almost a curse, dividing the nation, buttressing every kind of absurd superstition, encouraging miraculous appearances – one was almost upon us at the time of which I am writing, and it paralysed the country for weeks – producing a special race of genuine tyrants called Parish Priests, like no other clergy in any other part of the world. Canon Duggan was ours, totally incomprehensible in everything he did, from the appalling prayers before Mass, to his sermon, a truly remarkable sing-song performance. Everyone knew it by heart and that first Sunday most of it was taken up and loudly repeated, a sentence in advance, by a man beside me who turned out to be the local idiot. I was the only person who went to Holy Communion, and it was clear that my approach to the rails was unexpected and surprising. There was a special Sunday for that.

In my second month a skin disease appeared on me, a rash over the whole of my body, and a fortnight before Christmas I took it home to Radlett, where my mother cured it in a week with baths of Condy's Fluid. Faith works many miracles.

Four

That Christmas holiday in Radlett was the first period away from all obligations I'd ever had since I first had obligations. There had always been school and the dread of going back. Now that was over.

At this time my brother Will was living with us, and that too made a big difference to me. He had been invalided out of the Army about six months before the end of the war. Now he was working for my father he usually came home from London on a late train and I always sat up for him. We'd sit talking until two or three in the morning. I learnt a great deal from him; I also began to grasp that he was different from most other people; that the war had done some dreadful harm to him.

Every day there was some discussion about my future. My father could not take over Synone until after the summer, and something would have to be arranged for me. It was at last decided that I should go for a year to live with two brothers who farmed in the County Meath and had indicated to the Irish Department of Agriculture that they would like to have a pupil. Off I went with my father to Ireland.

Naturally we travelled third class and in great discomfort. Nowadays if I go to Ireland I go in all the comfort I can muster, not because I am naturally a sybarite or a spendthrift but because I still shudder at the memory of that journey. No one who has not travelled with my father knows anything of discomfort. A man may have walked from Katmandu to the first camps on Everest, he may have sledged across the Antarctic or the Greenland ice cap; he may have been the first man to burst into the Kanchenjunga Basin – but he is only a beginner if he has not travelled to Ireland with my father.

There would be first of all the meal at Euston. I had many such by myself in later years. I walked quietly into the hotel, was helped to a table by a waiter, selected a modest repast, ate it, paid and walked quietly out in the direction of the Irish Mail.

None of that would ever have done for my father. There would first of all be the speech, usually made while dragging bags along the endless corridors of the Underground. In this case we had come from Radlett and had, of course, to walk on the surface from St Pancras to Euston. The speech would go like this:

'There are men, my son, – that dilapidated outcast slinking past us as I speak and signalling for that cab is an excellent case in point – who would take a taxi for the few hundred yards of this simple walk. As that man obviously already has, such men inevitably come to ruin, the ship sinks beneath their feet.' Sometimes there was a confrontation. The man referred to would say: 'Are you talking about me, sir?' My father without hesitation would reply: 'I am, sir. I am using your obvious failure in life as an object lesson for my son here. He is my youngest son, my Benjamin, expensively educated, about to cost me more than I can reasonably afford, but a young man of account, a young man who cannot be considered a dud. You sir, to whom I now wish good night, are not such a man. You are essentially a man of *no* account. Good night.'

But this time there was no confrontation. My father however was disturbed by the fear that I might want a meal. 'It is better before journeys involving transportation by ship to refrain from heavy eating, to make do with a snack. We will have a snack at Euston, my son. It will get you through. Your mother has perhaps not sufficiently hardened her sons but a snack will get you through.'

In vain to hope for a porter to relieve one's burdens at Euston. 'Idlers, my son, to cut a dash, to make a figure, hand their luggage to porters, demeaning the hireling to bolster their exaggerated opinion of themselves. Such men prefer to live in a mews in W1 to an establishment in, let us say, Stamford Hill; they are men of no account. Take my bag, my son, select two corner seats in a non-smoking compartment, while I get our tickets and decide about refreshments.'

The night mail to Ireland was in those days a miserable affair. Today there is at least a chance of refreshment; there was none until after the Second World War. Home-going Irish labourers however provided themselves with adequate liquid refreshment. My father, as I have already mentioned, was a total abstainer. In our drink-filled compartment there was an outbreak of singing well before the first stop at Rugby. My father glanced about him and selected a victim. 'The British Government, having tried for centuries to turn our people into helots, hewers of wood and drawers of water, is about to reap a whirlwind of terror and destruction. Dragons' teeth, as I have often pointed out to my son here – my youngest son, my Benjamin as I often call him, a young man of perception, but lacking judgment, lacking an orderly mind, lacking a serious sense of purpose – dragons' teeth, I tell him, have, when sown, the disagreeable habit of producing crops of blood. The impending tragedy, which my son will experience to the full – I am taking him with me to continue his training on the land – the impending tragedy will not be lessened but increased and prolonged by the weakness of our people at present being demonstrated from this and neighbouring compartments. The curse of Ireland is not – and I say this with a full sense of responsibility, and with no specific reference to you, sir, at present taking a swig – I think that is the word a man of your sort would use – a swig of raw spirit from a pocket flask – the curse of Ireland is not oppression by the British, although I could talk for a while on such a point, but Drink. You sir, flask to mouth, are as far as I can observe merely bringing ruin to your wife and family. The men in the next compartment, now adding shouted obscenity and the threat of violence to their drunken revelry, are assisting their country along paths which can only end in disaster. I see you have the *Star* there. I was unable to obtain one at Euston, and perhaps you will allow me to glance at your copy.'

I never saw anyone hit or attempt to hit my father; I never heard anyone remonstrate with him, tell him to shut up, tell him to mind his own business, or in fact do much more than start agreeing with him, smiling with and not at him, helping him along his road. He had the most tremendous presence, and he exuded what today is called 'charisma'. I wanted no share in it.

On the boat my father made no attempt to secure a cabin. He had at least gone to the length of buying the sort of third-class ticket which permitted saloon travel on the boat. He made for the smoking room, put his bag on a seat, thought about a cup of tea, rejected the thought, put his bag under his seat, and composed himself for sleep for the three-hour crossing.

86

We were to spend the next day going to Meath for my interview, to come back to Dublin for the night, and cross back to England the following morning. We left our bags in the Westland Row Hotel, never since the night that followed to know my presence, and took an outside car to the station.

The brothers were kind and interesting. They had a lovely house and much beautiful farm machinery. Their whole farm was in grass, the machinery all connected, as I could see at once, with the cutting of grass, the grinding and mixing of purchased foods, and the needs of mixed livestock. Over a late luncheon they said what a pleasure it would be to have me, named the fee they expected, to which my father agreed without so much as a blink – he never grudged large sums of money – and drove us to the Dublin train. My father was in high fettle, slept like a log in our shared bedroom, through which, or so it seemed to me, trains actually ran all night, and was bright and fresh in the morning for the homeward journey. He announced to my astonishment that this was a different sort of journey and that we should be travelling first class throughout. 'The day journey, my son, is as the lark to the owl, all is bright and beautiful as opposed to, or in contradistinction' – that was the kind of word my father loved, and always repeated if he chanced upon it – 'in contradistinction to the gloomy view enjoyed by the owl which, unlike us, can see in the dark.'

The morning boat was delightful, a bright calm December day, and in the train at Holyhead a cheerful head dining-car attendant asked us which luncheon we would be taking. He was serving three, there being a big crowd on the train as far as Crewe. My father chose the third luncheon and, just after leaving Crewe, we were summoned to it.

'My Benjamin and I will drink water,' said my father to the table steward as he settled himself comfortably and took up the menu. 'We will both have the luncheon,' he said, 'but with my roast lamb I shall have boiled rather than roast potatoes.'

'Boiled potatoes are off, sir,' said the table steward. 'I have in my hand', said my father, 'a list of the food provided on this train for the benefit of travellers. Where my finger rests you will see clearly printed under the heading "Vegetables" the words: "Potatoes; boiled, mashed, or roast". I have indicated my preference for "boiled".'

87

'They're off, sir,' said the table steward. 'Plenty of roast, and a scraping of mashed. Not a boiled potato on the train, sir.'

My father laid down the menu. 'You are not to be blamed,' he said to the table steward, 'and I do not propose to bandy words with you. The shape of your head, your general configuration, if I may so put it, indicates that your position here is subordinate. There will be a head man in this coach, a man akin to that centurion who remarked to our Lord that he was a man subject to authority, having under him soldiers. You will recall the passage, I have no doubt. Ask the gentleman to step this way.'

The courteous head attendant who had reserved our places for this ill-starred feast bowed to my father. 'Something wrong, sir?' he asked.

'No,' my father said, 'nothing is wrong, nothing is wrong at all. There is a trifling misunderstanding, a misunderstanding which a word from you will clear away as though it had never been. It is suggested to me that boiled potatoes are off.'

'That's right, sir,' the head attendant said, 'finished as we came into Crewe. Plenty of roast, sir, and I could find you, I'm sure, a portion of mashed. But plain boiled, sir, no.'

My father held up the menu. 'Then this document misleads. It is clearly stated here under the heading "Potatoes" that potatoes boiled, potatoes roasted, and potatoes mashed are available. I make my selection and you inform me, that my selection is void, nugatory, not to be entertained. I must insist that you are mistaken. I must insist on a portion, a fair and reasonable portion, of boiled potatoes.'

'They're off, sir,' the attendant said, 'there aren't any. I can't serve you with what I haven't got, now can I, sir?'

'I imagine', my father said, 'that there is a yet higher authority on this train. I have been told by someone, possibly your Chairman, a difficult man, frequently wrong in his political opinions, but nevertheless a man familiar with the day-to-day working of a railway, that on every train running upon the London and North Western Railway – and I have no information as to the comparable situation in say Italy, a country which otherwise I know well, France, Germany now lying crushed beneath our collective allied heel, or indeed the trans-Siberian railroad between Moscow and Vladivostock – that on each and every one of our trains, in one of which I am now seated, the guard is the supreme authority. You might care to summon him on my behalf.'

I had reached the end of that particular road, and got to my feet. The table steward, the baffled head attendant, my smiling urbane father – I could stand no more of them. 'I don't feel well,' I said, groped my way out of that accursed car, and made my way back to our compartment. It was restful there and, all desires purged, never wishing ever again as long as I lived to eat or drink, I sat looking at the fields rushing past me. Just after Watford, with the beginning of the end in sight, my father appeared in the corridor. He was smoking a cigar, he looked well and happy. He opened the door and sat down. I didn't speak. I didn't feel like it. But he told me. 'They boiled me some potatoes,' he said.

Two days later came a letter from the brothers in Meath. They had thought about it, they said, and they didn't think they should take on the responsibility of me. They led a lazy life on some of the best grassland in the world. All I would really learn if I went to live with them was how to buy cattle in the spring, leave them alone all the summer, and sell them fat in the late autumn. All they did in the winter was to hunt and shoot. It did not seem to them that their life should be encouraged in a young man with a living to make. They were sorry.

So it was all to do again. Another round of letters brought another round of replies, one of them in answer to an advertisement which my father had put in the *Irish Times*. It was such an amusing letter that my father wrote about it to his friend in the Irish Department of Agriculture. My father's friend in the Department was interested. The man who had replied to the advertisement was without question the best all-round farmer in Ireland. He was certainly in no need of a pupil; there must have been something in the advertisement which had appealed to him.

My father wrote to Mr Willington, of St Kierans, Birr, King's County, Ireland, that same night. By the following morning he had arranged for me to be fitted out completely with various types of country clothes, and to go over to Synone, once more, for a few days with Mrs Nicolson. He would follow with all speed, would meet me at Ballybrophy, and we would go together to Roscrea for an interview. Mr Willington's letter had ended: 'I'd have to have this young genius in the house for a night or so before committing myself to a year of him.' I knew from that why I had not been shown the advertisement in the *Irish Times*. No doubt the word 'Benjamin' appeared in it. There must have been something to amuse them all at St Kierans.

In a week I was off, with most of the things I would need for a year, including a bicycle. Mrs Nicolson's daughter, Haddie, met me at Thurles, sitting up behind 'Brownie'. Haddie had a sick woman friend in the trap with her and I bicycled along behind them. Everything was already familiar except the burnt out police barrack at Holycross. The state of Ireland was getting worse, but no one was particularly worried about that. It had always been possible to manage the Irish.

I stayed four or five days at Synone and set off for Ballybrophy to meet my father on what must have been the coldest January day for fifty years. Jack Heffernan drove me in from Synone to Gooldscross to pick up the mail train. The little station was crowded with people; someone was going to America, someone who would never come back. But as a policeman in Boston, or a farmer's wife in upstate New York, that someone would perpetuate in the United States a hatred of Britain in Ireland which is with us still. Of course I didn't think about that then. I was interested in the weeping girls, the keening unhappy old women, the crowd of men all with too much drink inside them. It was the custom then to put fog signals on the lines as the emigrants left, and I began my short journey amidst shattering explosions, shrieks of despair from women, and from the men the high 'Tipperary Yell' – a sound to frighten bishops. After that it was a quiet uneventful journey.

I had three hours to wait on Ballybrophy station, which is some twenty miles from Ballybrophy village. The little book-stall was open, there was a small refreshment room. I bought a book and sat happily reading, eating sandwiches, and now and then getting the girl in charge to 'wet a fresh cup' for me. I had begun to know and to like the slow easy ways of Ireland.

The Dublin train came in at last, and there was my father laughing and chatting with a large man he had met in Dublin, the man with whom I was to spend the rest of the year. He was dressed, on that coldest of nights, as he was always dressed, in ill-fitting tropical-weight breeches, plain leggings, a tropical jacket, open and buttonless, over a cotton shirt of cellular material, with a loose black silk tie round his neck and an old felt hat on his head. I could see at once that he was very much my father's idea of a man, and that he thought the same of my father.

'This is him?' Mr Willington said, shaking hands. 'That's him,' said my father. Nothing more was said to me, and we got into the waiting icy cold two-carriage train waiting to take us to Roscrea, and thence by a still smaller, still more antiquated train to Birr. By the time we reached it I was frozen to the bone.

Mr Willington's Ford stood in the dark of Birr station yard waiting for us. It was a 1913 model which in due course left its marks upon me. It was of course open; it took about half an hour on those early Fords to get the hood up properly and the task was only attempted if the weather was set for a month or two of rain. Tonight it was only freezing, and we set off for the twelve miles to St Kierans, my father in front with his new friend, me in the back. Before we were clear of the little town I was crouched on the floor.

The lights failed on Gallows Hill, a mile out of Birr. That was to be expected; the lights on early Fords were a miracle of improvisation, waxing and waning with the engine, but usually not working at all. We stopped long enough for Mr Willington to put a match to a stable lamp which he asked me to hold over the side, and we were off again. I had no gloves and thought my hand might drop off before we reached our destination; I have never been so cold since, even wading in deep snow on mountains.

Six miles out we drove into a herd of cattle on their slow way to the fair at Birr the following morning. The crash was tremendous, our unlighted lamps crumbling into powder, a bicycle being wheeled along by the leading herdsman a wreck beneath our wheels. Mr Willington was on the road in a flash, abusing the front and rear herdsmen by their first names, recalling their wasted lives from the moment they had left the national school in Rathcabbin, roaring for the cattle to be got out of his way. As we drove off he called out: 'Get the bike repaired and send me the bill.'

The house, a big stone Georgian house, two floors set above a vast basement full of servants, was at the end of a long drive. I had to be helped from the car, almost frozen to the back of it, my lantern arm dead to the shoulder. Mr Willington and my father were now men who had known each other for many years, my father's Benjamin a forgotten cipher. I was introduced to Mrs Willington, whom I thought quite terrifying, immensely English, immensely cold. I was introduced to Ivy, a little girl of ten, and to Malcolm, a soldier home from the war, badly wounded, and with a Military Cross. He was bigger than his father.

We dined and Mr Willington left us with Malcolm while he withdrew with Mrs Willington to the drawing room for night prayers, the great unbreakable ritual of the house. The four of us sat in silence, Malcolm, my father, Ivy and I. After a bit Ivy went to bed, Malcolm got up and went out of the room, I huddled over a huge turf fire, my father read a book, astonished that this lonely house was ablaze with electricity. In half an hour Mr Willington returned and I was sent to bed, my fate unknown.

It was a damp bed but I soon warmed it, and it me. I slept without moving and was called at half past seven by a maid with a jug of hot water. At breakfast, nothing was said about me, my father answering endless questions about creameries, bacon factories, the state of Ireland as he saw it, Synone, and the future of everything. I knew we were to catch an early train for Ballybrophy and my father's return for an afternoon in Dublin before the night boat bore him away for a year. But no one spoke of me. At the end of the meal Mr Willington pushed his plate away, looked at my father and said: 'I'll take him, but not to make a cheap labourer of him. I'll take him to learn a bit of management. I like him.' In fact, we liked each other until he died. He named what in those days must have seemed an enormous fee and my father smiled at him, nodding 'Of course'. It was all settled in five minutes. I said goodbye, was told to be back to stay within a week or ten days, and we went off in the Ford to Birr. That time I had only two hours to wait at Ballybrophy, but they were lonely hours. I was a little afraid; I was about to be plunged into a new world.

Jack Heffernan was at Gooldscross to meet me and I went to Synone, this time beginning to feel like the owner to be, telling Jack of St Kierans and the big man who owned it. Of course

Jack knew all about him; there are no personal secrets in Ireland. But he said nothing; he was still employed by Mrs Nicolson. At that time we thought that I would be in residence and in charge of Synone by the following Christmas, but he had not yet transferred his allegiance. In fact, it was a few years before I came back to Synone and began to learn wisdom from Jack Heffernan.

It was the middle of January, 1919, when I left Synone for St Kierans. For the first time in my life I had a little money in my pocket. My father had liked Mr Willington. I was to be all right financially all the time I was with him.

Life at St Kierans was strange for me and went on being strange. Here I was, a young man of nearly eighteen, alien in religion and education, isolated within the Protestant Ascendancy.

Mrs Willington had a passion for animals and a dislike for most human beings, including her son Malcolm who had come safely home from the war leaving his elder brother dead in France. She could not forget her eldest son, or forgive Malcolm for surviving. All the same, I came to love everyone at St Kierans. In the first place, I was regarded as an intelligent person in my own right. At my very first breakfast Mr Willington asked for my opinion, Malcolm made a joke when I gave it, everyone laughed. I seemed to fit in. For the first time I had the right clothes. I had boots, leggings, breeches, flannel trousers, jackets, suits, proper waterproofs, and I even had some money. I needed it less but I had it; loose pound notes, a five pound note, the promise of more if I asked for it. 'You are going to a house where you will need to keep up an end,' my father said. He knew about that; he had kept up an end all his life.

'First things first,' said Mr Willington after breakfast. 'We must go into Birr and make you a temporary member of the County Club.' So into Birr we went, past The Pike, a group of crossroad cottages where no two families were on speaking terms with each other, past Dulanty's forge and implement sheds. They were Protestants, enjoying the dangerous patronage of a doomed race, but happily not knowing it then and waving gaily as the old Ford clattered by. We passed Colonel Head's Derrylahan Park; he was later to fly for his life down his back avenue as the revolutionaries drove up from his main gates to burn his house. Past Gallows Hill, past Booterstown with a Union Jack flying from a private house, soon to be destroyed, and into the main square of Birr.

We entered the King's County Club, and went straight back to England. Everyone present, English, Irish, Scotch or Welsh was British to the core. In the smoking room lay the Irish and English *Times,* the latter soon to be banished for disloyal tendencies and to be renamed the '*Daily Mail,* for twopence'.* There, too, lay the essential papers for Irish rural life – *The Field,* the *Sporting Times,* the *Winning Post,* the *Shooting Times, Horse and Hound,* and *Country Life.* The only books I ever saw in the club during my year of membership were a complete set of *Ruff's Guide to the Turf.* The essential priorities were properly observed in the King's County Club.

The great military barracks, intended for Malta but accidentally erected in Birr, had already been gutted by fire. The whole country was alive with troops rushing about in Crossley trucks, and there was talk of an Auxiliary Force being created. We were soon to become acquainted, but not during my first months, with the Black and Tans, one of the last Great British Mistakes. None of that was thought of on my first morning in the King's County Club.

Mr Willington would not allow me to sit in the bar. My fellow members I met only at luncheons at St Kierans or elsewhere. We all moved about in a tightly closed circle, but I was kept away from the possible evils of drink.

I had a very pleasant room at St Kierans and I spent a lot of time there. I could read at night because we made our own electricity. Family prayers were the signal for me to go to bed, and as they were held at nine thirty I always had a long night in front of me. So I read a lot, many books about agriculture and farming, but also books of another kind. It was at St Kierans that I first read *Resurrection, Anna Karenina* – and much else of Tolstoy. I read all of Fielding and anything else I could find in the house. 'You read too much, Fitz,' Mr Willington used to say.

I grew friendly with all the servants in the house, Sarah and

---

*The *Mail* cost a penny, *The Times* twopence (in the days of 240 pennies to the pound).

Bridie and Mollie, Tom Rourke the coachman, and Mike O'Ryan the carpenter. Mike used to get drunk once a quarter, following a strange unalterable ritual. First he would disappear from the house and his carpenter's shop. It was no use looking for him then; three days had to pass. After that, the search could begin; this house and that cottage were visited by Mr Willington and me. Word would finally be received of 'the whereabouts', and we would pick him up, shattered right through. The rest of that day, and all the next, he would sit in the kitchen drinking pot after pot of black coffee and, a week to the minute after his disappearance, he would return to his carpenter's shop, ready to give me a little lecture on the wickedness and evils of drink. "Tis a kind of a class of slavery, that's what it is. Never begin it, never be talked into just a glass that will do no harm. Hell lies there.' It is indeed 'a kind of a class of slavery', and for too many people Hell still lies that way. But I drank water in those days, had never tasted so much as a glass of beer, loathed the smell from the open doors of public houses.

We went out shooting a lot, until the end of the season. All I did was to carry the game bag. Both Malcolm and his father were marvellous shots, hardly ever missing at snipe or wood-cock and never at driven birds. But a couple of hares at the beginning of a long day of snipe shooting on the bog are a thousand hares at dusk, after miles of bog walking, wet through, tired out, and all the time trying to pick up agricultural learning from the talk.

Mr Willington was without any question the best all-round farmer in Ireland. As a breeder of Large White pigs he had no superior in Europe. He knew more about tillage than most men, could win prizes with his Aberdeen Angus cattle, could weigh a beast by eye to a couple of stone, was a judge of barley. His knowledge of farm machinery was unique in the Ireland of that time; he was a barrister too and his every word was gold dust for me. He never liked me to do much farm work, although I loved doing it whenever the chance came, but I could write down today his whole philosophy of farming. He never hurried; he never worried about the weather. 'There is always a seed time, always a harvest,' he would say. 'Learn to wait for it, Fitz.' He would never rush on to wet land, never put the binders into damp corn, never overwork his horses because it was fine.

95

He remains for me the perfect example of the perfect farmer. He spent enormous sums on drainage, on controlling water, on what everyone called totally uneconomic pig feeding. 'It's odd, isn't it, Fitz,' he used to say, 'I win all the prizes at all the shows, get the top price and a bonus from the bacon factories, make a lot of money from my pigs, and yet I'm doing it all wrong.'

He laughed a lot. Sitting at the head of his table at breakfast on a wet morning, no work possible, 'raining ruin', as my father used to say, he was at his best. 'Put on a pair of shoes, Fitz,' he would say at the end of the meal, 'and come to Birr.' Off we would go to play billiards all day in the club, coming back after tea with the groceries, the *Irish Times,* and the letters. But I would also come back with a great deal of mixed information about the life history of badgers, or the secret of throwing the half-hundredweight, or why S. F. Edge was wrong about open-air pigs. The rain had not ruined me.

That spring things in Ireland began to go seriously wrong. Mr Willington was a magistrate, and I would go with him to local courts. The police carried rifles in court and no one dared to give evidence if the case had any political or 'land' context. Mr Willington was marvellous on the Bench, making everyone laugh, putting everyone in a good humour. But other magistrates in other courts went beyond their duty to express their patriotic adherence to British Ideals. Colonel Head would hold forth about thugs and rapscallions and he was followed by half the magistrates in Ireland. There began to be night raids for guns, and all holders of guns were advised to put them into police barracks. All our good guns, which stood in the hall when I arrived, were taken into Birr and safety, leaving only an old non-ejecting hammer gun, weak in the left barrel, with which I used to go out after pigeon. Then at midnight the raiders came even for that. But they did not burn the house. Magistrates began to resign, but *not* Mr Willington. He knew, we all knew, that no one would shoot him. But they did try to shoot Colonel Head, and were very sorry to miss him. They burnt his great stone house to a shell, giving Mrs Head five minutes to get out of it with the children, and allowing nothing to be taken from it.

I liked Colonel Head; I could beat him at lawn tennis, the slow garden-party tennis of those far-off days, fish-tailed racquets, yellowing white trousers, red rubber soles on soft brown leather shoes, the grass too long, the net too low, everyone happy. He bred a great many poor quality Herefords – 'white heads like the children,' he used to say – had a charming and very brave wife who struck the captain of Irregulars when ordered out of her house as her husband fled from immediate execution. 'I could have you shot for that, madam,' the captain said, 'but I won't. You have courage.' But Derrylahan Park went up in flames that night and has never been rebuilt, the land divided, the 'Whiteheads' gone.

Things got steadily worse. In the kitchen Tom Rourke the coachman preached the Dawn of a New Age in which the Workers would take over Ireland and the Bosses would cry for mercy. His activities were interrupted for a time by the appearance of Our Blessed Lady to a half-witted boy in Templemore; his statue of the Sacred Heart had dripped blood, a fountain of Holy Water had sprung from the floor of his cabin. All Ireland rushed to the spot, except the Dean of Cashel, Monsignor Innocent Ryan, a voice crying in the wilderness. 'Keep away from Templemore,' he begged everyone. ''Tis an idiot boy and I know him well.' In vain. Special trains were run, 'jarvies' (drivers of outside cars) began to make fortunes, there was a brisk trade in stones from this holy spot, to be taken home to those who could not travel. Many of these stones came from no further away than a wall on the farm to which they were being taken. It all died down overnight. 'Bad luck to the Dane of Cashel' was on the lips of every jarvy, and Tom Rourke went back to preaching the Revolution. Towards the end of summer he had formed a local agricultural branch of the Irish Transport and Workers Union and declared one morning, at the window of the breakfast room, that work on the farm had ceased, that the gates were picketed, that the Dawn had come. Without looking up from his bacon and eggs Mr Willington said: 'Get your things out of the house, Tom, and never come back; you're finished here.' 'There'll come a day,' said Tom, going away. But there never did for him: he had been thirty years in the house.

During the strike there was a lot of work to be done at St Kierans. The horse men were 'out', and Malcolm and I fed the horses at dawn every morning. It was a wet harvest year and we had endless trouble with the corn. A six-acre field of Spratt

Archer barley, being grown experimentally for the Irish Department of Agriculture, lay out, every sheaf being reopened and retied by hand twice, until November. We were at it all day; we had to plough out potatoes a row at a time, cart them in, pit them, and start all over again the following morning. We had to run the gauntlet of the pickets every day. They took off their hats, said 'Good morning', but sometimes turned us back. We always went back; Mr Willington would not allow us to fight. Gradually the strike fizzled out but it lasted for more than three months. It wasn't about money; the men were offered that. It was about a new heaven and a new earth, promised by Tom Rourke and not delivered. Mr Willington paid me a full agricultural wage all the time the strike lasted. I had never had so much money in my life.

My father left it to Mr Willington and his friend Charles Going to fix the Synone live and dead stock valuations, to be paid to Mrs Nicolson. Prices were high, bullocks at sixty pounds each, barley in the stacks at sixty shillings a barrel of fourteen stones, heifers at forty to forty-five pounds. And a year later, when they belonged to my father, thick, fat, bullocks, after a winter's stall feeding, were fetching twenty pounds apiece. Barley was unsaleable at thirteen shillings. My father lost £20,000 on his purchase that first year.

That was still to come. I went home to Radlett for Christmas, after a happy year at St Kierans, with the world at my feet. I was a man, I was going back to take charge of Synone, there was not a cloud in the sky.

It didn't last. Ireland was ablaze, men being shot and killed every day, bombs and burnings every night, girls tied to chapel railings, their hair shorn, their bodies covered in tar and feathers, men on the run, men 'out with the Brigades', men being taken out of bed to be shot, taken into gaols to be hanged, the whole dreadful process so familiar over the centuries. England has never learnt that there is only one Irish problem, England.

There was to be no Synone for me in the spring of 1920. Instead, because 'it would soon blow over', I was to go to an agricultural college, 'for a term or two', to pick up a few technical hints. We looked at prospectuses. At last we decided that the new and beautiful Seale Hayne College in the heart of Devonshire was obviously the place to go. I was to go for a term only to take the short certificate course and to leave for Ireland in the autumn. In fact, I was there for four years.

While my father was corresponding with the principals of various agricultural colleges, it had become too late for the current term of Seale Hayne. To fill in time, I went as a general mechanic and learner driver to the George Bowles Garage under a single arch of the vast Waterloo Station train approaches. They operated as carriers for my father's business. In that dreary and rather dangerous part of Lambeth, I learned that women do actually fight each other, a horrid sight when they arrived at the no-holds-barred stage. They liked to tear each other's clothes off as a starting point. Then they would go for each other's hair, breasts, and eyes. My colleagues liked it. 'Go it, mother,' they would shout, or ''it 'er again, Gert.' But I was a bit soft.

I used to catch what was called in those days 'the workman's train', from Radlett, take the Tube from King's Cross to Lambeth North and walk from there. It was strange going to London in farm breeches and boots, my mother's daily half crown in my pocket, and with my 'workers'' season ticket. Mostly I read *The Times* in the train but once a week, as became a professional, I read *The Commercial Motor*. I went on long delivery trips, 'the Awley and Crawley', 'the Sarfend and Greys' and there were long waits in Surrey Commercial Docks or Hay's Wharf to pick up hundreds of the two-cheese crates from New Zealand. I sometimes forgot the back end of the lorry when driving and once took off the end of a bridge as I turned sharp left. But there was little real traffic about in those days and no one saw or heard me. 'Just get out of here, Duke, nice and quick,' my mate said, and out we got.

Grocers were our natural enemies and to this day on the rare occasions when I enter a grocer's shop, I am filled with suspicion and apprehension. In those days, we would swagger into a grocer's shop with our 'way books'. 'Good morning, sir. George Bowles, sir. Four crates New Zealand finest white, four boxes Anchor butter, two boxes Skibbereen Irish Creamery, three picnics [those were tiny hams] and a box of English butter rolls. All right, sir?' Then the grocer would say, 'In the cellar, my man', and we would go back to our wagon, let down the tailboard and unload.

We usually had to listen to a lecture on poor quality, on idlers like ourselves being always late, on the state of the nation, owing to people like ourselves never doing any work but driving about the country like lords. And then: 'You can take back last week's side of Irish bacon. Disgraceful, sending out goods in that condition', and we would be shown a side of bacon with all the best cuts gone. We knew the claim would be for a whole side. The claims clerk in 'the house' said that all grocers spent Sundays working out and putting in claims. 'Our turn', they would say, 'comes about every two months. Just pick up the stuff, that's all, Duke.'

When the grocer had signed our way book, always 'uninspected', the best of them would give us twopence. I was never allowed to keep my tips. "And it over, Duke,' my mates would say, 'Guv'nors' sons get nix.' 'Nix' of course was not what they actually said. They were splendid chaps, my mates. On their days off, they would come into the garage in their violet suits – that was the 'in' colour then – and sharp brown shoes, laughing and talking and taking the mechanics out for drinks. I still didn't know what beer tasted like.

Naturally I didn't get any days off and I would stand at a bench-vice listening and laughing with them and endlessly skimming away at a soft metal shaft-bearing with a 'reamer'. Every so often you 'blued' the bearing, slipped in the shaft and turned. The rough places carried away some of the blue and you reamed on and on at the new marks. I expect there's a better way of doing that now.

I didn't get paid, which was why my mother gave me my half crown lunch money every morning. With this I bought myself a point steak at a nearby 'Slater's'. They were restaurants for working men and clerks, but there were waitresses even there. I always left mine sixpence, not realising that the going rate was a penny, and when my time came to leave and she asked me what I had been doing all those weeks she wouldn't believe that I had been working underneath the arches. 'You throw money about,' she said. Well, there's an Irish saying:' It's bad to be poor and it's bad to look poor. But to be poor and to look poor is the Devil all over.' I suppose I've always tried to avoid that.

The Lambeth garage was very different from my recent Irish experiences, standing beside Mr Willington waiting for driven birds at Portumna Castle, sitting by the auction rings at the Royal Dublin Society's March bull sales, lording it at the May Spring Show and the August Horse Show. But I got over St Kierans by letting it flow over me into oblivion. And I had learnt while I was there how to calve a cow, how to pump up a milk-fevered udder, how not to keep farm books, how not to cost farm operations, how to harness various kinds of horses. I knew how to plough, which gave me the edge on the boss; he didn't, and envied me greatly. Above all I learned a sort of patience. I didn't learn his special brand which was a unique and private property, but I did learn a sort of patience, a knowledge that if you waited, things would come right. I learnt that there is always a seed time, and there is always a harvest.

They hadn't learned that at Seale Hayne where I was going. When I arrived only five of us had ever spent any time at all on a farm. Even the lecturer in agriculture hadn't.

When I arrived at Newton Abbot station, in early May 1921, I felt happy and released. I knew how to snag turnips, string a binder, plough with a pair of horses, feed pigs, milk cows, and look in the right direction when trying to judge the weather. I had a trunkful of clothes and books, five or six pounds in my pocket, and no idea at all about 'agricultural education'.

The Seale Hayne College was a vast red and white building, brick and Portland stone, standing high on the skyline. As a college, it had made a first start, then been stopped by the war, and was only just beginning to get going again. The staff were new, the students were new. I had a pleasant room. It was quite large, had a bow window, a bed, a table and a chair. The porter told me that curtains, comfortable furniture, and anything of that kind would have to be bought by me. A manservant would make my bed and keep the room tidy. I asked him how many students there were and he though about fifty so far. 'But we haven't really got going yet.'

Seale Hayne was, I suppose, much like other places of the kind. That first evening of the summer term, people began to drift in one by one. Someone asked me if I played cricket and seemed disappointed when I told him I was no good. Eventually about thirty of us answered a dinner bell, rung by a man in a black jacket and striped trousers, a sort of P. G. Wodehouse butler. The meal, 'a meat tea', was everything conveyed by those words. I never got used to it, could never eat it with enjoyment. It was to lead me into trouble.

Late that evening a large notice board outside the porter's lodge was filled with timetables. There were lectures on practical and theoretical agriculture, lectures on forestry, botany, agricultural chemistry, crops, livestock, poultry keeping and the growing of vegetables. There were periods devoted to farm walks, cheesemaking, buttermaking, the cow shed, the forge, and machine management. There was a list of the staff and their subjects.

The next day, the official opening day, was free from work, but I visited various staff members, as I was asked to on the notice board, and I walked into Newton Abbot with lists of books. It was one of those books, *The Soil,* by Sir Daniel Hall, that introduced me to that mythical character – that fabulous monster – the totally serious Scotsman. *The Soil* is an unreadable book if ever there was one, though a book I needed and have always valued. But soon my astonished ears took in Mr Mackintosh declaiming that no novel ever written could compete with *The Soil,* that the earnest student would make its revealed wonders his day and night companion, that all that mattered to human life on this planet was to be found within its pages. I began to discover that specialists in the academic world hardly ever stray outside their subject. What Mr Mackintosh did not know about soil, bees, pruning, and pollination was not knowledge. Outside that he was pretty long on the metrical psalms, the Waverley novels, and the other usual impedimenta of Scottish intellectual life; he recited 'The Cotter's Saturday Night' but frowned on the lighter love poetry of Burns. It was unhealthy, he thought. All the same, I liked Mr Mackintosh very much and was sad when he killed himself a few years later.

The college was 'shaking down' after a sticky start and so were the staff. The Head of the Agricultural Department was another dour Scotsman who left almost at once, to be succeeded by a man called Troup, a most delightful character with a Russian wife who sat about on floors in immense pools of black velvet looking like a pearl in a midnight oyster. The Chief Agricultural Lecturer began all his lectures with the words: 'In practice on the farm . . .' It always seemed to me that he had managed to avoid any of that.

Then there was Miss Amos, straight up and down in black silk, the Matron, and her friend, Miss Crosse of Poultry. Down in the dairy was little Miss Ireland. And there was a collection of farriers, farm carpenters, and someone called 'Shep', a character straight out of musical comedy who actually wore an embroidered smock and carried a crook. But he did not last long.

After Mr Willington and St Kierans, the whole of the college farming pattern seemed ludicrous to me, small-scale operations in tiny fields, conducted by men brought up on Scottish farms and wondering (as I did myself) how on earth you harnessed a pair of horses to that strange West Country device, the Turn-wrest plough. This was an 'under and over' machine to avoid ploughing round and round a 'back' on really steep land. Instead of that the ploughman remained in his furrow, turning the horses really sharp and twisting the whole plough over to reverse the direction of sod. It was interesting but difficult to learn. And I could not get used to the hideous South Devon cows, ungainly creatures and the wrong colour to go with grass.

The Principal, Lieutenant Colonel D. R. Edwardes-Ker, was the new postwar breed of man. He had a degree from Oxford and another from London. He played lawn tennis for Devon County and he possessed the Grand Manner. I suppose we were not ready for that, but personally I came to like him. He knew a lot, and he wore it lightly. Most of the staff in my first term were more concerned, it seemed to me, to tell us how much they knew than to make any attempt to get some of that learning into us. But before I got to know him, I was to have a terrible encounter with the Principal which nearly ended my career at Seale Hayne.

The first meeting of the Seale Hayne Union Club took place about three weeks after the beginning of term. On that hot summer night in 1921 we assembled in the Refectory to form a Union Club. We were, the Principal said, as he took the chair, to elect a President and a Committee. We would become responsible for the 'tone' of the College, all its internal affairs as they affected us as students, and would put forward recommendations and suggestions to himself and through him to the Board of Governors. We elected a President and an Editor for a magazine. The Principal departed and a general discussion began about what we thought the College should be like.

Someone said something about the food. Someone else said it was appalling, dogs would flinch from it. I asked what could be done. The Chairman said he was prepared to lodge 'the general feeling of the meeting' with the Principal. I asked what was the good of that. The Principal would say that he would look into it, would have a word with the Steward, who no doubt would have a word with the chef. I said that a better idea occurred to me. At the 'meat tea' next evening, as the servants came in with plates of disgusting sausage meat, we should sit in silence until all were served and then, on a signal from our Chairman, rise and hurl the contents of our plates – not, mark you, the plates – at the Steward as he stood smirking by the doors to the kitchen. He would, I suggested, look pretty ridiculous standing there covered with sausage meat in front of the staff at High Table. He would be unharmed, and we would have made our point in a way which could not be ignored. There was laughter and some cheering, but it was decided to leave matters to the Chairman. It was all rather fun and rather enjoyable and we broke up affably. and went to our bedrooms.

The following day I was asked if I would make it convenient to call upon the Principal in his office. I think I rather expected to be asked my opinion on one or two practical matters. His secretary told me to go in, and there I was on the first of the many office 'mats' on which I was to find myself as I fought my way through life.

Edwardes-Ker was a tall, immensely handsome man and he smiled upon me. I smiled back. I am even now constantly smiling at men holding concealed knives which they are about to drive into me.

'FitzGerald,' he began 'you are Irish, I think.' I had not yet grasped that this is the typically British beginning to particular forms of insult. 'You are Irish, I think' is a useful all-round opening for 'You are dirty; dishonest; seem to have acquired some unpleasant habits; are a Catholic, militant Protestant, red revolutionary', or anything else which the speaker dislikes. When I answered the Principal that, yes, I was Irish, he went on:

'You are also, I gather, a dangerous Bolshevik.' This seemed a trifle extreme and I said of course I wasn't, and why was he saying that. I was very polite, using the word 'sir' a lot, and feeling a bit worried. He was stern and unyielding. 'My information is that you made a highly charged inflammatory speech at the Union last night, suggesting, nay, urging, an attack on our most excellent Steward and endeavouring to create here the kind of atmosphere which this country is now putting down with absolute finality in the country from which you have just come.'

I said it was not like that at all. That I hadn't just come from Ireland, although my father owned land there. I had come from Lambeth where I had been working in a garage. 'Where you have clearly picked up some very dangerous ideas,' he said. He went on to say that he understood that I had received my education at the most exclusive Catholic School in the world, that surely the schoolmate of the Duke of Norfolk, the Lord Dormer, the Viscount Southwell, the de Traffords, the Scropes, all the old English Catholic families, was not trying to import into this peaceful Devonshire enclave the kind of regime which had destroyed the Romanoffs, produced Rasputin, created a bloodbath in Eastern Europe. I began to see that I was going to be sacked. I stammered out something about thinking I was making a cheerful speech about nothing very much, that people had laughed, that no one had actually done anything. 'FitzGerald,' he said, 'you are that detestable and dangerous animal, a silver-tongued rogue and agitator. There is to be a short meeting of Governors within the hour, prior to their Annual Luncheon; the First Annual Luncheon, indeed. I have decided that you will have an opportunity to state your case before them. If they think as I do you will have to leave us, FitzGerald. That is all.'

I hung about for the rest of the morning until just before lunch when I was 'called in'. There they all were, filling the Principal's office. One of them became a lord, one lived in a castle, one was President of the South Devon Herd Book Society; they all looked grand and intimidating. The Principal introduced me and they began to ask questions, beginning of course with: 'Colonel Edwardes-Ker says you are Irish.' There I stood, hands behind my back, in the attitude of that boy in blue velvet who was being asked when he last saw his father. The inquisition went on until suddenly a stout lady intervened. 'Mr Principal and gentlemen,' she said, 'we are making ourselves ridiculous. It is perfectly obvious to me that this handsome [that's what she said] this handsome young Irishman is a gentleman, with the habits of one, and with an extremely amusing face. I wish I had heard his speech; I feel I should have been won over, and have thrown my luncheon today at our Steward. I suggest that we ask Mr FitzGerald to go away and return to his studies. Let us caution him of course, and remind him that life here is a grim and serious business into which no comic relief must be allowed to enter.'

Everyone laughed, and I was told to go. I was saved only by Miss Calmady Hamlyn, a famous breeder of Dartmoor ponies, long dead I suppose, but never forgotten by me. I only saw her once more over the years. She was walking across the quadrangle after a meeting and our paths crossed. I bowed, and she smiled: 'Ah, the Bolshevik,' she said, laughed at me, and went her way. I wish her well, wherever she may be.

The term dragged on and I gradually began to feel at home. A feature of life in the College was Saturday morning examinations, and at the first of these I scored a success. There was one question: 'Write an essay on the oat as a crop'. I knew a lot about that and wrote for two hours without a stop. Lo and behold, next Wednesday a notice went up on the board announcing that I had been given full marks. But I don't think I ever did that again.

I worked very hard indeed. At eleven o'clock the College lights gave a warning flicker, and ten minutes later the Warden began an official tour. If any room light was on he knocked and asked the reason. The only excuse accepted was work. My light was always on; I was always working, though sometimes on a book which I pushed hastily under Hall on *The Soil*.

My father's affairs were once more in crisis. There was no money for me and we were not going to have much of a holiday. Suddenly everything brightened and an air of deep mystery developed; we were going over to Ireland. It seemed a bad time to be doing that but nothing came of it. Once again we were penniless and once again I was a young man who had half a crown in his pocket if his mother had one to spare.

We were now temporarily in an enormous flat in London. I had good walks and talks with my brother Will and I went to stay with Vaughan at Radlett. But everyone at Radlett was in business and running to catch trains. No one but me was interested in agriculture. I wanted to go back to Synone but Ireland was ablaze and it seemed out of the question. And so early in September, back I went to Seale Hayne.

The whole atmosphere was different, a host of new people arriving, all looking interesting and amusing. Would I play association or Rugby football? I loathed association football, and I put my name on the board for a Rugby practice.

There were several people from good Rugby-playing schools. I found the first practice was enjoyable, and soon I was picked for the first fifteen and stayed in it for the rest of my time at the College – which turned out to be much longer than anyone had expected.

Five

It became clear that Ireland was going to be out of the question for at least a couple of years, and I gave up the short certificate course and enrolled for the National Diploma in Agriculture. This was awarded after a strenuous examination by the Joint Boards of the Royal Agricultural Society and the Ministry of Agriculture and Fisheries. The course took three years and demanded a full year's work on a farm as a precondition of entry. That of course I had done.

There were various interludes during my time at Seale Hayne. During one summer vacation I went to Denmark, to a farm in Jutland owned by Mr Ladefoged, a friend of my father's. There I worked with the men but slept in the house and was expected to eat Danish blue cheese for breakfast, washed down with pints of jet black home-brew. I couldn't do either nor could I manage the usual luncheon soup which had soft eggs and cheese floating about in it. Mr Ladefoged was very kind to me and asked me to his sixty-fifth birthday party, a function which gave me a respect for Danish men and women which I have never lost. We sat in a huge marquee, and I was next to the prettiest girl in the tent. She had never been out of Denmark but spoke perfect English. Everyone there had three bottles of wine placed in front of him or her and the first shot was fired at five-thirty p.m. – tea time in England.

We were still in our places, still eating and drinking, at three o'clock the following morning. By that time all the women, including my beautiful girl, were smoking gigantic cigars, an unusual sight then, but no one was showing the faintest sign of being over-eaten or approaching intoxication.

There was no main drainage in that remote part of the country, and every bucket and Elsan closet was overflowing long before midnight. I learned a lot that night about the needs of the human body; it seemed to me at one time that every bush for acres had a woman crouched behind it, or a man standing beside it. I don't remember going to bed; perhaps I didn't.

On the journey home, I ran out of money – as was to happen to me all my life – somewhere about halfway across the North Sea, but I had a comprehensive first-class ticket to Liverpool Street. We arrived there on a Sunday and I betook myself, very late, to St Pancras (for Radlett), where I stayed the night in the vast gothic Midland Hotel. In the morning they refused my cheque, drawn against the inadequate allowance my father had started to give me. I pleaded, the clerk was adamant. He was right, of course. In those days no one offered cheques without weeks of previous letter writings and personal bank credits. But I had met a nice man on the boat who had told me in the train from Harwich that he was the Danish Consul in London. I asked the hotel to telephone him and describe me. They did and he guaranteed my cheque. I wrote and thanked him and in his reply he said I had an honest face and had used the ladies' lavatory throughout the journey in the ship. This, he said, was not the conduct of a potential confidence trickster. I suppose he never realised that I thought 'Damen' meant 'for men'.

If I. B. Prowse had never come to Seale Hayne I think the rest of my life might have been different. Certainly I should not have developed an interest in David Jones.

Prowse had been at Tonbridge and, I think, he finished up a master there. He was in our first fifteen as a full back and, although he had never got into the Tonbridge fifteen, he was I think the most stylish and – until J. P. R. Williams, of Wales – the bravest full back I ever saw. He wore spectacles but held that a man couldn't get hurt in glasses if he tackled low enough. He was also a rock climber, a breed about which, at that time, I knew nothing. He made a route on the Great Boulder at Chudleigh as early as 1922 or '23. He also liked climbing about on the local quarries, circling rooms by the picture rails, making the traverse of billiard tables, all nonsensical behaviour to me then. He said one day that I was an ill-read man. I challenged this and he spelt out a list of absolutely essential books. I had read none of them. I began to put that right the same evening and have been trying to catch up ever since.

One night Prowse handed me a small book. 'It's about a horse race,' he said, 'you'll like it.' It was Masefield's *Right Royal* and of course I liked it, just as I liked *The Everlasting Mercy* and *Reynard the Fox* and *Dauber* and *The Widow in the Bye Street*. I don't find them all that readable today and they aren't the current literary fashion, but everyone who reads or speaks English should have snatches of Masefield in his head along with more respectable quotations. After a year of Prowse I had neglected a lot of dull agricultural reading but I was at least well up in most of the English classics. That's important if you are to make anything of David Jones, particularly when you come across a passage like:

> He shifts his failing flanks along the clammy slats, he settles next his lance-jack, he joins that muted song; together they sing low of the little cauldron, together they commemorate *Joni bach*.

Well, you'd need to have played Rugby football with Prowse, to have read somewhere that at football matches the Welsh always sing 'Sospan Fach', and that the reference to 'Joni Bach' means that the pussy cat has scratched little Johnny. You ought to know, too, something of the Arthurian legends, and what is meant by the Triads. And all you have actually read is a short passage about a soldier of the First World War moving down a trench to join a singing comrade.

And it was also because of Prowse that I knew Dunbar before Jones and that I came to know Hopkins and the difference between sprung and standard rhythm. It was all very heartwarming. Prowse was interested in music as well; he lent me money against the arrival in the bank of my allowances; he discouraged my developing interest in the girls of the neighbourhood, and was altogether what my parents would have called 'a thoroughly good influence'.

He couldn't have guessed, though, how much more was to grow out of what he actually introduced me to. Poetry is an acquired taste, like Scotch whisky. And he taught me how to sip, and to go on sipping when I liked it. He left the College much too soon. He wanted to take a B.Sc. in Agriculture which I never found did much for anyone, other than to substitute a knowledge of enzymes for a love of the plough. And, of course, to help people to invent ways of doing without ploughs altogether.

There were other interludes during those years at Seale Hayne when I was supposed to be learning to farm. For three months I lived with my widowed Uncle Tom and went with him every day to his work. He was the secretary of the big, London-based, provision-importing company of which my father was chairman. I was in danger of failing in book keeping in the final examination for the National Diploma in Agriculture and my father paid me two pounds a week, all through the long vacation, to be a junior in the invoice department of this company, spending nearly twelve hours a day – yes, nearly twelve hours a day – doing incomprehensible things in triplicate books. Each set of three pages had to be lined with carbon paper and backed by an aluminium plate before, if you were me, you began writing in indelible pencil: 'Coop Soc Devizes, Four crates (4) white NZ at 112/-.' You had a huge ready reckoner book in front of you, and did all your sums from that. Between three and five o'clock in the afternoon a couple of ledger clerks, very superior men indeed, came into the invoice office with the middle sheets of the innumerable 'triples' you had made all through the long day since seven a.m. These corrections you had to transfer to the top copies which then went off all over England with the goods. At six, or perhaps half past, Uncle Tom would appear, still in his office slippers and black alpaca coat. 'Dear boy,' he would say, "Coop Soc Devizes is not the way to address the manager of the Co-operative and Agricultural Society of Devizes, Wiltshire; nor is "white NZ" a sufficient description for "New Zealand White Cheddar Cheese, Finest Quality". Are you ready? We'll start for home in half an hour.'

It was marvellous, living with my Uncle Tom. He talked like a book all the time. He never made an arithmetical error of any kind, he knew everything about the provision trade that there was to know and, when general motor transport came in, he knew all about that in less than a month. 'All lorry accidents, dear boy,' he would say, 'are caused by devastating collisions between two or more stationary vehicles.' My father thought his brother-in-law rather stupid and had only given him the job because of my mother. Everyone else knew better. My brother William was a director of the concern, which rambled all over Smithfield, and because of his war experiences and the mark they had left on him, he lived virtually on the premises in a private house my father had caused to be made from some semi-abandoned offices in Hosier Lane. Like the rest of us, my brother worked late and long. My father strongly disapproved even of Saturday afternoon closing but had to come into line with it round about 1921. His own day in the office began at half past ten or eleven, but his personal secretary and half a dozen other people nearly always missed the one evening train they particularly wanted to catch.

My uncle was meticulous about grades in business, about courtesy and formalities, even among relations. Once when we were leaving for the train from Holborn which took us home, I said: 'Will's bint's still in his office, Uncle.' My uncle stood leaning on his umbrella looking at me: 'Dear boy,' he said, 'never again on these premises are you to refer to Mr William's secretary by the term, "Will's bint".' He always called my father 'sir' during the day, and so did I after I'd charged into his office one afternoon in my ink-covered white coat shouting that it was a bloody shame allowing his workers to be ground down by foremen and sacked for losing things off the backs of wagons.

On Sundays my Uncle Tom came into his own. He was a most deeply religious man, which explained to me why he had been engaged five times before he married my Aunt Agnes. She thus had six engagement rings after her wedding, nearly always wearing the lot. Mother told me that once when he was quite young, Uncle Tom fell in love with a girl he kept meeting in the street. Every time my uncle passed this girl he would stop, looking back at her until she was out of sight. One day, weeks and weeks after the first encounter, he forced himself to say, 'Good morning'. The young lady tossed her head and called out: 'You poor bloody fool.' 'That was in 1886, dear,' Mother said, 'and young ladies weren't supposed to talk like that in those days. I expect she felt goaded. Girls do sometimes.'

But on Sundays Uncle Tom was Master of the Ceremonies in the Augustinians of the Assumption Church in Brockley. During the week, his housekeeper, Agnes, would cook our breakfasts overnight and lay them under tin covering plates on top of the gas range. During the week we got up at five, put our two plates on top of two saucepans to warm them up over hot water, and caught the train from Chatham at Crofton Park which got us to Holborn just before seven a.m. But on Sundays Uncle Tom went to Holy Communion first thing and Agnes had breakfast freshly cooked for all three of us by the time he got back.

After breakfast Uncle Tom went in majesty back to church to take charge of everything. Priests did what they were told, read the Collects he had marked and relied on all his missal ribbons. Choir boys were totally subdued. Everyone, from cross bearer to thurifer, assembled in spotless cassocks and surplices; the priests were all properly vested; all waited to hear Uncle Tom tinkle his tiny starting bell and say 'Now'. Then a solemn procession entered the church from the sacristy and made for the sanctuary.

That was why on Saturday nights there was a special 'doing' of Uncle Tom's boots. He liked the insteps blacked and the soles smoothed. 'A congregation sees a lot of the undersides of a kneeling man's boots, dear boy,' he used to say. I did them for him because I had been to a very exclusive and expensive school where, though I learnt virtually nothing else, I was beaten a great deal until I had learnt to clean shoes, whiten cricket boots, polish military equipment, and do things with tins of condensed milk which surprise me still.

In the choir of the church at Brockley there was, as it happened, a young London Welshman called David Jones. He had not yet written *In Parenthesis,* but he was to startle my Uncle Tom, who never understood either the poetry or the prose of David Jones. Here was a man he saw at Mass every Sunday suddenly appearing as a writer, a painter, a poet. Everyone knew that young Jones had never been more than a lance-corporal in the First World War, and that had been over for years. Who was this quiet, rather holy, London Weshman to produce a book, and an unintelligible book too, with a strange picture in front of it which they said he had painted himself? After all, he was only a clerk or something in the City.

My Uncle Tom couldn't understand the book or the picture, when they did appear, and was floored altogether a few years later by *The Anathemata* which he found quite meaningless. I wasn't there at the time but I know what he would have said. 'We weren't sent into this world, dear boy, to understand everything; it's time to do the boots for church.'

I was an appalling invoice clerk, complaints reaching the 'House', as it was called, from every quarter of the country within a week or so of my arrival. But my uncle was determined that when I took the Diploma Examination I should pass in book-keeping if I failed in everything else. And he succeeded. At the book-keeping 'viva' held in the University of Leeds, the examiner said: 'You have managed to reverse the correct procedure in every possible case in your written work, but, in a manner which is quite beyond me to explain, you demonstrate an excellent knowledge of the underlying principles.' I told him that I owed everything to my Uncle Tom and said I hoped he would pass me. 'And so I shall,' he told me, breaking all the rules.

Because I was the Chairman's youngest son I was finally allowed to spend a fortnight in the ledger department. Before the arrival of mechanisation, the ledger department of any business was holy ground. It was the last court of appeal for anything to do with 'the Accounts'. In his office, and in office hours, the ledger-keeper was God. His clerks had to be with him for years before being allowed to make an actual entry in the Sacred Volumes and once a matter in dispute had been 'turned up in the ledger', that was the end of the affair. 'The ledger cannot lie' was the rock on which every sound business in the country was built. Its production, or a sworn copy of a sheet, in any court of law was enough for any judge, and the appearance of a chief ledger-keeper in person would satisfy the House of Lords itself.

Mr Wood kept our ledger, and I can see and hear him still, dead these last forty years. Someone, having opened a grocer's shop in, say, Kensington, would call to 'open an account'. He might well have references from the King's grocer, who was one of our customers, or from that world-famous shop in Piccadilly which was another, but up to Mr Wood he would have to go. And over and over again I heard the sequel. 'All very good, sir, and one I'm sure we'll be proud to have over the years. But in the meantime, sir, oblige us all by making it cash. All our travellers, sir, and many of our carmen, are armed with our full authority. For the time being, sir, you make it cash.'

Mr Wood, a stately figure, arrived at eight a.m., an hour after Uncle Tom, who liked to 'supervise the post'. This meant the opening of hundreds of letters by four young men under the direction of Miss Bradley. It was said that once, many years before my time, when my father was making City history by employing women and installing telephones, a nameless boy had managed to steal a postal order under the very eye of our then young Miss Bradley. But that had been a lesson and a shame to her. Now she was our elderly Miss Bradley and no such thing was feasible; the very idea of it was ludicrous. Besides, if you stole anything, there was first of all my Uncle Tom and then Mr Green the chief cashier: 'Nothing for it, son. Straight up to the Governor,' and that meant my father. There were people there who told me that they would prefer long terms of imprisonment to entering his office at the directions of Mr Green for a financial offence. I can believe it.

When the post was opened, Mr Wood would take charge of its general distribution. At post-distribution time Mr Wood would be in felt slippers, an old black alpaca jacket, false cuffs, and fully equipped with a battery of special pens. No one was allowed to approach the ledger, the volumes of which took up the entire main wall of Mr Wood's kingdom – you couldn't call it an office – unless they could write proper 'clerk's hand' with a proper pen. No fountain pen was ever seen, let alone used, in the ledger department. The post would be distributed – money to Mr Green, hundreds and hundreds of orders to their various departments, complaints to Uncle Tom, thick cream laid envelopes from the Vestey Brothers, or Swifts, or Armours, all marked 'Chairman only' to my father, many others of only slightly less richness to the partners or other directors. After that, Mr Wood would begin his real day. Just before three o'clock, but never a minute earlier, he would 'go out to lunch'. He was back in ten minutes and there would be a faint, very faint, odour of Scotch in the ledger department. Mr Wood never ate in the daytime but he always had one drink 'just before they closed'.

Things were different about drinking in those days. There

were gradations; there were men who 'drank', men who spent 'rather too much time drinking' and men who 'liked a drink now and again'. Men who 'drank' were undoubtedly what nowadays would be called alcoholics. There was a lot more drunkenness visible on the streets. It was a commonplace in Smithfield Market, for example, to see men who had had too much to drink going about their ordinary work, and many of the clerks in the surrounding warehouses 'took a drop' in the middle of the day. The odour of Scotch emanating from Mr Wood after his daily luncheon break would arouse comment today. It passed unnoticed then. My father would have noticed it, but he never visited the ledger room; that would have been resented.

If Mr Wood felt that some big credit customer was entering a period of risk he would consult my Uncle Tom and Mr Green, the cashier, and then pay a state visit to the Chairman's office. Then his voice could be heard as far away as the ham floor. 'He may well be a lord, sir, but my concern is not with the House of Lords, but with this House. And this House, sir, should begin to think in terms of cash when next we get an order from his lordship.' Mr Wood could do something no one else could do; he could, just a little, cow my father. 'The ledger can't lie, sir,' he would begin 'and the ledger says that from taking a regular ninety days' credit his lordship has crept up to a hundred and ten, a hundred and twenty days. That's a suspicious circumstance, sir. You have a word, sir, with the town traveller when he comes in on Saturday. You tell him that of course it's nice to get a big order for every one of his lordship's chain of shops and that we don't even mind delivering a picnic ham, and spending four times its value in the process, in an empty two-horse van with a boy on the back as well as the driver, to a shop the other side of London. But you tell him that for that trifling service we would like to be paid oftener than once or twice a year. And good afternoon to you, sir. And thank you for the honour of seeing me.'

No one in the house was ever optimistic about 'expenses' or money. Mr Green was as reluctant to hand an 'average clerk' half a crown to cover a day of 'outside' activity as he was to pay an expense sheet covered with approval signatures. He and my

Uncle Tom shared a low view of practically everyone in the provision trade.

'I have seen a boy', my Uncle Tom would say, 'with, on his jacket, a gold badge indicating that he was something called a Knight of the Blessed Sacrament, such a boy as that I have seen extract a postal order from a letter with the kind of skill which a conjuror might envy.' Mr Green was gloomier still. 'This cheque,' he would say, holding the piece of pink paper delicately between two fingers, 'this cheque is coming back to us. This cheque wears a lie on its face. This cheque is not a gentleman's cheque. When a gentleman signs a cheque, sir, he hands you a bank note. No such person has signed the document in my hand at this moment. I must have a word with Mr Wood.' And off he would go, but not before putting away every scrap of paper visible behind his grille and double-locking the door of the office. When it came to human nature, and what everyone was capable of, my Uncle Tom, Mr Green and Mr Wood were in a class by themselves. If the words 'make it cash' were engraved on the heart of Mr Wood, the words 'there's something wrong with this payment' were on Mr Green's. And not even Miss Bradley knew quite what to look for on Uncle Tom's.

Miss Bradley was almost the first, if not the very first, woman to be employed in a London business. My father had the curious belief, not even now generally accepted, that women were people, people with immortal souls, with hopes and fears, and above all with brains. Miss Bradley was popularly supposed to be in love with my Uncle Tom, and a department manager, far gone in drink, had once sworn that he had heard Miss Bradley say 'Good night, Tom' late one evening, as she left the office. No one believed him. Miss Bradley – her skirts sweeping the ground, her face set in determined lines of distrust, suspicion, disillusion, and undeviating devotion to the House – was the personification of all that is meant by deportment, correct behaviour, frugal living and no outside interests.

There was another of the 'early girls' who was the purest gold dust too. My father was deaf, and from their earliest days had difficulty with telephones. He still regarded Mr Edison's and Mr Bell's invention as 'new-fangled' right into his last years, after the Second World War. But he knew he must come to terms with it, and there was a complicated multiple switchboard in the House as soon as it was possible to get one. It was the highly trained Miss Beale who worked it. She and her switchboard were built into a cubbyhole behind my father in his grandeur. His own telephone, with a gigantic rubber listening piece to fit right over his ear, defeated him quite often. Then, immediately behind his head, a little trapdoor would open and Miss Beale would tell him what was being said. She knew all the secrets and never told one.

Miss Beale also knew my father. No one entered his office without 'testing the water' with Miss Beale. 'Don't ask him for money today,' she would say to me. Or 'I'd leave all that, Mr William, if I were you; he's dreadful today.' She must have known all the criminals, all those who had been found out, all the hard luck stories. But she never told anyone anything.

One day, I was trying to get Mr Green to cash one of my cheques and he was pointing out, not too seriously I am happy to remember, that he would feel better about it if my father wrote his name on the back of it, 'with his private address, Mr Kevin, so that it doesn't come back to *me'*, when the most frightful uproar broke out in my father's office. His door was only shut when his business was of the most private kind, and it was shut now. But his great voice would have carried through battleship armour plate, and through an ordinary door Mr Green and I could hear every word. 'Emily,' he was shouting at Miss Beale, 'come in here at once. At once, Emily: I wish you to hear, witness, and recall, that I have twice called this visitor a liar and a knave, and that before he leaves me or I summon the police I wish him to be assured that I shall welcome his action for slander. Sir, you are a liar and a knave.' Mr Green paled, and I fled. Later I asked Miss Beale who it was and what had happened. 'I don't know anything about it,' she said.

Miss Beale was wonderful, and I'm the only person of that generation who knew it for certain because, during my two-month book-keeping vacation, I asked her out to dinner and she accepted. No one then believed that business women were actual women. But they were. Miss Beale was twenty years older than I was and, fifty years later, I can remember where we dined, what she said, and how we parted. Pure gold, Miss Beale was.

During my last week with Uncle Tom I asked him if he ever thought of getting married again. 'Married again, dear boy?' he said, and I can still see the look of stupefaction on his face. 'Married again? Dear boy, I am doing what they all told me to do at your aunt's funeral, awaiting the will of Almighty God. In this matter, dear boy, He has been mercifully slow. Let us do the boots.'

After staying with Uncle Tom, I went back to Seale Hayne. Sometimes, even now, fifty years after I left, people ask me: 'What went on at Seale Hayne while you were there? What was it like?'

It was all very leisurely. We were either there on county grants or because our parents could afford it. Few of us had any idea of what we wanted to do after we left. Every morning was devoted to lectures and two or three afternoons a week to laboratory work. But we had a lot of time off for games, for cross-country and road running. There was a good deal of motor bicycle activity, some quite serious rowing on the Teign, serious Rugby football in the winter, desultory cricket and lawn tennis in the summer, much 'binting', as the pursuit of local ladies was called, and quite a lot of us made serious botanical and zoological collections. In our second year, a lot of us began to work quite seriously for the National Diploma. I was one of them. In Ireland, the setting up of the Free State in 1922 was at once – and quite naturally as we would now think – followed by a civil war of appalling intensity. So it was the Diploma or nothing.

Veterinary surgery was a subject rather like Roman law; you could buy a shilling book and learn it by heart. I could still, asked about the functions of bile, expand the famous mnemonic into pages of examination prose. 'Bile from the liver saponifies fat/helps to absorb and emulsify that/Aids peristalsis and purges a bit/Prevents putrefaction and . . . gives the dung its characteristic colour.' But to make sure of enough marks on all the oddments of building construction, book-keeping, agricultural chemistry, zoology and the like you really had to do some work. 'Working, FitzGerald?' the Warden would ask, knocking at my door at 11.30 p.m. 'Alas, yes, sir,' FitzGerald would reply, passing a hand over his brow and edging Prowse's copy of *Married Love* under some loose papers. 'Good night, FitzGerland.' 'Good night, sir.'

In the last year at Seale Hayne I had developed a certain standing. It looked as though I might be a successful student, actually securing the National Diploma in Agriculture, thus bringing glory to the Principal, his staff, and the college. After my shaky start I had at last become accepted in the Principal's house and I was often invited to tennis on his court, which meant being offered a glass of sherry – 'No, thank you, sir, I think I'd rather not' – or a tumbler of lemonade – 'Lovely, sir, just what I wanted.' I spoke to his pretty wife as 'Gypsy' and danced with his really beautiful niece. One night in Torquay she remarked: 'I could dance with you, FitzGerald, all night, every night, for ever.' She neglected to point out that she was also leaving the district for ever next morning.

On Sundays, I would often walk with a man called Morgan to Ashburton, have tea there, and walk on to Buckfastleigh in time to listen to the monks chanting Vespers and Compline in the great abbey that they were building. For Morgan and me Sundays were devoted to plain chant and the eighteen-mile walk to Buckfastleigh and back, with immense talks about life, literature and animals.

Both of us were devoted to Miss Ireland in the dairy. She was of course Scotch; all the best dairy girls were Scotch in those days. She had the roundest bosom I have ever seen and she knew a lot that mattered to Morgan and me. We were both eventually going up to Scotland for the National Diploma in dairying and it was interesting to chat with Miss Ireland about cheese, which seemed to be part of her religion, and to hear about a man called Drummond, a sort of Being from Outer Space, the greatest cheesemaker in the world, an inspirer of holy thoughts about cows and curdled milk. I had learned to dislike Professor Drummond long before I set eyes on him. When I did, I disliked him far far more. He was, take him for all in all, the most detestable man I ever met in my life, and I've met a few detestable men.

While at Seale Hayne I fell in love, a disastrous affair which went wrong from an early stage. She was what is called 'Very Highly Connected'. She was also very prim and correct, being rather more than outraged by my suggestion that she might care to accompany me to the local dance hall. No gentleman, I learned, ever asked a lady to 'one of those dreadful places'. This particular dreadful place was the converted Newton Abbot Picturedome, and it closed at ten p.m. precisely. Mothers sat round the walls keeping an eye on their daughters.

My grand girl had rather grand lodgings but worked in a solicitor's office; the solicitors managed the estates of her grand family. After my tentative proposal I got a letter on paper as stiff as Agamemnon's dishonoured shroud inquiring icily about my prospects. I replied warmly that I had no prospects pending a solution to the troubles in Ireland, adding that my talents and heart lay at the feet of their 'dear girl', as she was called on the stiff writing paper, that I would cheerfully work my fingers to the bone (I cannot possibly have left out that cliché), and that if ever a dear girl was adored to distraction this one was by me.

I never got an answer to that; all the same, we became engaged and I was a farm labourer in Canada when she 'broke it off'. She had been staying with my parents in Ireland and my father might have put in an oar or two. She kept the ring but sent back the books lovers send to each other.

I've usually been a bit unfortunate about books to girls. I tend to think they are going to like *Practical Cheesemaking* or David Jones's *Anathemata*. They don't always. Thirty years after that I saw her once more and gave her lunch in the Ladies' Annexe of my club. She was wearing my ring round her neck in an affecting manner, but all it did was to remind me of my Uncle Tom. His girls always gave back his rings, but God knows mine hadn't cost much.

By this time I was living in lodgings in Highweek and working at the College all day. I had lodgings which everyone else thought were clean and comfortable. I now know a great deal about clean and comfortable lodgings, quite enough to avoid them. After agreement has been reached on terms and length of stay, bags moved in and beds approved, there will be a revelation about a bucket lavatory or the absence of running water. Sometimes someone called 'our Lil' is mentioned. She will be described as 'quite harmless, poor dear,' and an assurance is given that noises in the night should be ignored. 'Dad and me are always able to deal with her.' In Highweek I had both Lil and the bucket. There was also an acute shortage of money resolved by visits with a suitcase to a pawnbroker in Torquay.

The pawnbroker became a friend and I learnt a great deal from him. I'm too old now to fake an old ivory box: 'probably about 1703, or a bit later, off an East Indiaman I shouldn't wonder; might have once belonged to a servant of the East India Company coming home with his fortune. Mind you, sir, I wouldn't like to *guarantee* it, but you can see for yourself that it's a very nice piece.' But I could still get you to look at a master-piece in oils. You'd have picked it out from a pile of old canvases at the back of my shop, and you know that it's by Vandervelde and you know just as certainly that I don't know that. 'I wouldn't like to say, sir. That's been knocking about the back of this shop for twenty years and more; left me by a friend, it was. He thought it was worth a fiver, but I've never been offered anything for it. Would I take ten pounds for it? Well I wouldn't like to say, offhand, sir. But you come in tomorrow and we'll see. I'll have had a word with my brother by then, he knows about pictures of ships and that sort of thing. Will I take twenty-five pounds? Well, of course I will, sir, but you'll be robbing yourself, you know. I only meant my brother deals in pictures and might have thought seven or eight a fair price. But twenty-five pounds? You'll take it right away, sir? So you shall, and I'll do it up nice; I've got a lovely piece of brown paper in the back somewhere. But I'm afraid I'm robbing you, sir.'

We passed hours like that, and after a bit he never bothered to open the suitcase or give me the official tickets. He would dump the case under the counter and give me five pounds. Then, when I had my allowance money, I'd come back with it and the interest, pay him and collect my case. He thought I had 'just the face for the antique and pawning. You've got that shining hon-est look, worth a fortune in the trade. If ever you strike it rough, come back to me.' Perhaps he was worth the bucket lavatory in the noisome shed, 'our Lil', and the walk every day to and from the College.

There was the final. Leeds again, and at long last the short list of Diploma winners was put on the big notice board. My name was on it and I sent a telegram to my father.

There was a fresh plan for a summer in Ireland, a summer

which eventually cost my father scores of thousands of pounds, but the most wounding part of it, to him, was the twenty pounds I cost him on my way to the holiday. There was a great Secret, so Great and so Secret that I knew nothing about it. He had bought me a motor car, one of the new all-black Fords, a big advance on the standard 1913 Tin Lizzie. But he did not tell me the car was for me. It was, he said, a car which I was to help take over to Ireland for a friend of his in the motor trade whose son would be coming with me. We could take turns at driving and the son would explain how Fords worked.

It was thought that the journey might take a couple of days, and I felt brave and comfortable as we drove through the village of Dunstable, and got ourselves on to what is now the A5 but was then Watling Street, the Roman road to Holyhead. I had the National Diploma in Agriculture; I knew practically everything there was to know about everything. I was on my way to the thousand acres of land which were to be mine as soon as Ireland calmed down a bit. My mother and father would be there to greet the hero as I drove up the avenue to my inheritance.

We had a puncture somewhere and what with one thing and another thought we had better stop the night at an hotel. We got away from that comfortably enough and made for Shrewsbury, where on our way into the town I hit a policeman. He was on the English bridge which in those days was a beautiful and almost deserted artefact bearing a large notice, NOTHING TO BE OVERTAKEN ON THIS BRIDGE. As I drove on to it the only other occupant of the bridge was a girl on a bicycle. I tried to slow the Ford and failed. It was very easy to accelerate when attempting to slow those evil machines. I swerved past the girl to save her life. A policeman walked into the centre of the bridge and held up his hand. He stood his ground and jumped a second too late. I hit him only a glancing blow, while I was reaching behind my back and pulling on the hand brake. That stopped us in less than a hundred yards and I walked slowly back to the beginning of what might prove a ten-year sentence. I smiled bravely on the policeman and inquired after his health. 'I'll see your licence just before taking your life,' he said. I handed him my licence and he studied the name on it. It took him some time. After a little while he said: 'Read me out that lot.' I read out, 'Kevin Columba FitzGerald.' 'You'll be a foreigner,' he said. I denied it. 'I am a British subject,' I told him, 'I hold a British passport. I am on my way to my parents in Ireland for a holiday.' He was a very nice man. 'You can expect anything from the Irish,' he said prophetically. 'Get over there as quickly as you can, get out of Shrewsbury immediately and never let me set eyes on you again.' I thanked him and got back to the car.

Much later that evening we were strolling through the town and there was my policeman in plain clothes. 'I thought I told you to get out of Shrewsbury,' he said. I admitted that, and explained that we had to stay the night in order to arrive in Holyhead at the proper time for the boat. 'I pray to God this town is not struck by lightning or suffers an earthquake in the night,' he said.

We got to Holyhead early the next evening, but you could not in those days think in terms of 'drive on, drive off'. The motor car was still a dangerous device. Every last drop of petrol had to be drained from the tank, papers signed exonerating the shipping line from all consequences of explosion, shipwreck, loss of life, hazard by casting away, bottomry, piracy, acts of God, and much more. Men had to be tipped to push, wheel, manoeuvre, scratch, dent, and finally chain down your vehicle, and then you would be told that maybe tonight, maybe tomorrow the vessel would sail. Ours sailed after breakfast the following day and finished up in a remote berth off the North Wall in the port of Dublin. It was night before we got the car out of the ship and found someone to go in search of a can of petrol. There were of course no petrol pumps. You bought sealed green tins which were opened by twisting the stoppers with the bottoms of other sealed tins. The whole thing was a sport rather than a means of travel. We spent that night in the Royal Hibernian Hotel.

The journey down to Synone was very difficult indeed. Synone is about ninety-five miles from Dublin, but we covered nearly a hundred and fifty that day in order to get there. The civil war was barely over, every bridge in the country had been blown up, everyone carried planks and with their aid crept across dangerous gaps over rushing torrents. There are no dry river beds in Ireland; every stream is alway in full spate.

We had the warm welcome I expected and next morning, the 'secret' out and the car mine, my father said, 'I expect it cost you a pretty penny to get here, five or six pounds I shouldn't wonder.' I said: 'Just over twenty-three pounds actually; I began to think that your twenty-five pound emergency float wasn't going to be enough.'

My father raged. He had fathered a spendthrift, a man to whom money was so much waste paper and base metal. For the money I had spent idling my way across England in a cloud of banknotes, men had worked themselves to death in mines, seamen had braved the perils of the Atlantic, negroes in South Africa had toiled below ground for weeks on end, farmers in Australia had undergone droughts, sheep-shearers in New Zealand had tolerated hunger and thirst. What all those men put together had laboriously earned in months of heartbreaking toil I had flung like roses into a whore's lap. 'Fitz, dear,' said my mother, 'don't say "whore's", and don't go on.' My father went on, but he knew he was licked.

It is only fair to say that when my father had finished he really had finished. He never bore malice, he never imputed unworthy motives even to the actions of the unworthiest of men; he never sat in protracted judgement; and in his rough, patriarchal way he loved us all. He certainly loved my mother, and she him. He had good family rules and kept them. He never, for example, asked to read, or inquired what was in our letters to my mother. 'If you are in serious trouble she will tell me and I will do what I can. But there are oftentimes [he liked words like 'oftentimes'] matters which children will discuss with their mother and wish kept from their father. I understand that.'

I once asked him what on earth a young man could or should do if he picked up some frightful disease. He never even paused for thought. 'I know what my sons should do,' he said. 'They should come straight home where they are always wanted. No one else wants a case of venereal disease anywhere about them, so if you get it,' – and here he gave me what is called in Ireland, 'a chainy look' – 'come home, my son.'

That rather bad day was helped along by Miss McTigue, our housekeeper found for us by the Willingtons. Peace had been restored, my father was bland, and we sat down to lunch, Mother, my sister Carrie, my father and I. Ever afterwards that day was called 'The Day of the Penaud Sardines'. In the ordinary way, and in accordance with ordinary family life, it would have gone down as 'The Day Kevin Brought Home the Ford', but the Penaud sardines won by several lengths. It appeared that they were more expensive than other sardines. They were an extravagance. By the time my father had gone through the whole history of the French sardine-fishing industry, had rehearsed the difficulties of tinplate manufacturers, had brought to mind the sins of fish wholesalers, particularly those engaged in the continental trade, selling canned goods to avaricious grocers and provision merchants, the sky was dark indeed. It had actually begun to rain and Carrie had left the table before Mother, who only two hours earlier had rescued me, felt strong enough once more to intervene. 'Fitz,' she said, 'until this very day I liked sardines. Now I hope never to have another sardine in the house, wherever that may be. It is clear that we cannot afford a motor car, a tin of fish or this huge ugly house, which I begin to wish I had never seen.' It was the moment for Mother's ultimate trump card, played at fairly long intervals, but never failing. 'One of these days I shall run away from you all: I would prefer to beg my bread from door to door, and I will, rather than go through another of these scenes.' My father laughed, as he always did, the atmosphere cleared, we finished our sardines, my father called for another tin to be opened, Carrie came back, Miss McTigue stopped crying, and peace reigned.

All through that holiday, cargo ships full of cheese, week by week, every week, were setting out from New Zealand for London loaded to the Plimsoll marks with my father's cheese. And as they crossed the Pacific, entered the Panama Canal and faced the Atlantic gales, the price of Finest White New Zealand Cheese fell week by anxious week, down and down, ten shillings at a time, far below the price at which my father had bought it. If ever a House that Jack Built went wrong, that speculation did. He had bought the whole output of whichever of the two New Zealand islands produces cheese. He had bought it before the cows had conceived the calves, whose birth would bring the milk, that would make the cheese, that came to beggar my father. But there was more.

My father had decided that the holiday should cost us nothing. It was to be spent in Ireland at Synone and he would have a small gamble in French rents which would produce at the appointed time the few hundred pounds to cover Ford cars for spendthrift sons, Penaud sardines for an extravagant housekeeper, his own first-class ticket, a couple of third-class tickets for Mother and Carrie, and a few of the page-long telegrams he liked to spend hours of every day composing. Before his little gamble in French rents was concluded, it had cost my father over twenty-five thousand pounds. That is the difference between spendthrifts and those who are careful with their money. Nor was even that all. The Synone overdraft with the National Bank of Ireland was to top the thirty-five thousand pound mark before his ship at last came limping into port. My father liked all that really. To him, it was the breath of life, but it explains why I have always paid my bills the day I get them, have loathed every moment of my long periods of debt and still try to keep solvent – even today in my eighties when I am living on borrowed time. Spendthrifts *like* to be solvent.

My father's telegrams made up long happy days for him. The black Ford would come out and I would drive him into Cashel, where the post office stood next door to the National Bank and thus both his main holiday interests were under his hand. He would spread out his correspondence all over the small available space in the post office and settle down in that remote Tipperary hinterland to demonstrate the Tycoon in Action. After an hour or two of earnest composition, he would produce for my Uncle Tom or my brother William, in far-off London, a money-saving document something like: 'Mackerel eating public avoid cheese eating summer months price falling no consequence recoupment autumn cheese eating necessity bankruptcy prospect courage Petain Scotts Marmion make certain all apprised desperation raining ruin FitzGerald.'

At the other end two or three baffled men would spend hours endeavouring to extract meaning from these money-saving messages. Once, during the holiday, we received a telegram from Uncle Tom who, four or five times in his lifetime, had a fine outbreak of blind rage. On this occasion, although he knew that there was a delivery charge of half a crown on all telegrams out to Synone, he did not prepay it. His message read: 'Your telegram completely incomprehensible stop. Please either write or send your instructions in clear Streatfield.' 'You've upset

Tom,' Mother said, standing with her hand outstretched for the half crown for 'Andy the post'. She did not tell my father that she would be adding a personal shilling.

My father was unmoved. 'One of the great difficulties of modern business', he said, 'is that it must be carried on, in large measures, in great part, by those trained in an earlier less speedy tradition. Your brother Tom, dear, doubtless competent enough in the clerkly skills, shorthand, pothooks, the compiling of accurate records of yesterday's activities, is out of touch with Today.' 'Oh, go along,' my mother said, leaving him to the intricacies of yet another telegram.

It was a relief to us all when that holiday ended, and a still greater relief to me that my father went off early. Carrie disappeared to stay with friends and pursue her Varieties of Religious Experience, and Mother and I were left together. That was to happen again, later on, for a whole glorious year. This time we drove about together on the deserted roads, went over to the Willingtons one day for lunch, went to Limerick and Clonmel. Mother was in her prophetic or Sibylline mood most of the time. 'No good will ever come to any of us from this place,' she said. That proved one of the major understatements of my life. It certainly brought no good to me, for whom it had allegedly been purchased. My father had already almost forgotten that and was to forget it completely within the next two or three years.

My mother and I had many adventures together. On one occasion we came to a bridge. There was just room for an ass-cart – they always left that when blowing up a bridge – to crawl safely across, and I had planks to widen my passage. I put these down, across the destroyed part of the bridge, and invited my mother to get out and walk across while I edged the car over. 'No, dear,' she said, 'if we are to go into the river we'll go together.'

I remember her too, on the way back to England, sitting with me in the mail train for Kingstown. We stopped at the North of Ireland junction in Dublin, then known as Amiens Street. She sat opposite me, her hands in her lap, bolt upright. 'How peaceful it all is,' she said, 'travelling like this.' Anyone who had ever so much as been on a bus with my father knew just what she meant. He would hold forth on top of a bus in his tremendous voice.

'We are passing the Poor Clares convent, my son. Dedicated women, saying your prayers and mine. I trust you have not abandoned the habit of morning and night prayer, a discipline in itself, a recollection that we shall all be called to account sooner or later, but a habit frequently, and as I greatly fear in the case of the possessor of so disorderly a mind as your own, sloppily performed and needing the assistance of those good women we have left behind us on their knees. There were no lights showing, you will have observed; they are frugal women, eating no meat, sleeping on the boards which will contain, as crudely put together coffins, their bones when life has passed. I observe, sir, that you are listening with some attention, closer perhaps than good manners would require, to my homily, addressed to my youngest son, my Benjamin. Unlike yourself he lacks the curiosity of the vulgar, and, if appearance be any guide – and life has taught me that it often is – he lacks that utter vacancy of mind, that total absence of thought, that lack of creativity which has kept you, and will continue to keep you, in subordinate positions. Perhaps you will be kind enough to transfer your unwanted attention elsewhere. I suggest that your idle gaze from the window, unseeing, unobserving, will present you with no insuperable problem. As I was saying, my son . . .' Yes, the peace came home, alone with Mother during that short stop at Amiens Street.

I went back to Seale Hayne for part of the summer term of 1923 and I spent a few days on a cheese farm in Kirkcudbrightshire. My father thought it would be as well to 'Finish the Job Thoroughly' and I went up to Kilmarnock in July 1923 to work for the National Diploma in Dairying. I had thought until then that slavery had been abolished for a hundred years. I was to discover that Jamaican sugar slaves and Virginia cotton slaves had little to complain of; they had never 'come under Drummond' at the Dairy School for Scotland, in Kilmarnock.

It still baffles me that grown men and women should have put up with Drummond. He was a Canadian, a bully, and the best cheesemaker in the world. Of this there could be no doubt at all;

129

it was acknowledged by everyone. I have seen Professor Drummond walk into the Dairy School cheese room, sniff, and point to a vat. 'Run that,' he would say. He was always right; he could judge lactic acidity without any assistance from modern science. His staff were terrified of him; he could, they knew, break them overnight, and for no reason.

It was a tremendously severe syllabus. Fortunately, I had done all the book work before I came: that gave me a little time for sleep. We got up at 4.30 every morning and were expected in the Dairy School at five a.m. to take in the early milk. Our day, which began so early, ended very late, and Sundays were work-days too. Cows give milk on Saturday for Sunday's cheesemaking, just as they do on Sunday for Monday's. Every day we worked from five a.m. until midday, went home for lunch, came back for lectures or for cheese turning, cheese binding, and, if on Stiltons, for the eight o'clock 'scraping'. After about six weeks, girls began to break down and cry into vats, men began to wonder if they knew how to read. And all through the long morning the Professor's cry could be heard: 'All together, boys', as huge buckets of boiling water were flung about the floor and lines of male students with rubber squeegees mopped the boiling floods away.

I was soon thoroughly sick of the whole business and particularly sick of Drummond. Once or twice I cut the piffling afternoon lectures and persuaded conscientious Scottish girls to come to the pictures with me. They felt they were sinning in every possible way – by sitting in the pictures in daylight instead of sleeping in the lecture room like everyone else, worse still, by not *being seen* in the lecture room – by being tempted by me. It made a discouraging afternoon.

It had been decided that we would breed Aberdeen Angus pedigree cattle at Synone. They are still my great love as a breed. Willington bred and showed them and I thought I could do as well. I had been over to Ireland a few months earlier to the Royal Dublin Society's annual bull show and sales, and we had bought some excellent foundation stock and registered with the Aberdeen Angus Society, and now, while I was at Kilmarnock, came the Highland Society's great annual show, which that year was at Perth. The Dairy School was given one day off for the show. But I had legitimate grown-up business there. I could introduce myself to the Society's Secretary as a breeder of both Aberdeen Angus and Suffolk sheep. I decided that I needed two days and Murray, who was sharing lodgings with me, thought he needed an extra day too.

Murray and I stayed the night in Perth, in a decent hotel, and in great comfort. We needed breakfast in bed, the care of hand-maidens, and a little bit of strolling about being civilised. We returned to Kilmarnock to find we had been sacked.

We decided that I should beard the Professor for us both. He greeted me in his usual sneering way and asked what I wanted. I told him: 'Reinstatement, please sir.' He began to make a speech. It was well known that Murray and I were a couple of playboys, that I in particular was there as a 'member of the idle rich'. He had never once seen me with a serious look on my face, and he was, I might have noticed, a very observant man. We had been removed from time tables and notice boards because it was obvious that we were nature's idlers, creatures of privilege. This was a Dairy School for workers, the sons and daughters of poor farmers, men and women with a way to make in the world. He went on a long time. But, in the end, well, if it suited Murray and me to return and do a little idle work he could have no possible objection.

When at last he had finished he gave me his thinlipped white-faced smile of dismissal, but I had not quite finished, standing there in my white apron, lovingly embroidered in red 'Kevin FitzGerald' by Miss Ireland. 'You must look nice for the Professor,' she had said. I asked him if he was a betting man, and he looked at me as though I had liberated a black widow spider in church. No, he said, he was not. Had my question relevance to our present interview? He was famous for sarcasm. I laid him six pounds to four that I would get the National Diploma in Dairying, and that less than half of his precious hard-working students would come anywhere near it. He didn't take the bet.

Every candidate had to be able to make a Cheddar, a Cheshire or a Dunlop, chosen over the vat at random by the visiting examiner. The examiner was there at the five a.m. reception of the milk; he saw it into your vat and named your cheese as he did so; he watched you right through to 'chissetting', putting the cut and milled curd into the moulds. You had, the next day, to make butter under strict competition rules. Start with the soured cream, churn, add separation water, draw off, pat and shape, all within two hours maximum. It was a good moment when, as you stood beside your bone-dry sterilised churn, arms folded, competition butter made up into three different packs on your working table, the examiner said: 'You may go, 27.'

It came to an end. I survived the course and the examination, and I got the Diploma. Fifty-three of the seventy failed. I set off for Ireland with NDS and NDD after my name, if I liked, full of determination to remake the agriculture, if not of all Ireland, then most certainly of Munster, to win every possible prize for Suffolk sheep and Aberdeen Angus, and to be the most successful young farmer so far to stagger the world. With both eyes wide open and no fear of the future, I strolled quite unconcerned into one of those old-fashioned basket rat traps. There is no escape for creatures thus emeshed.

Six

It was a disappointment, my return to Ireland, loaded with the academic honours of that remote world of agriculture in books. I was engaged to my grand girl, I was going to change the world. But the autumn rains had succeeded the summer rains, harvest was dragging on in the Irish way, and after Kilmarnock, everyone seemed to be moving about in dreamland. My father was at Synone and it soon became abundantly clear that I was not to be in charge of anything. My wages were to be twelve pounds a month, my father pointing out, as he enlarged upon my good fortune in arriving so soon at such a high rate of pay, that, living at home, having board and lodging free, being about to be rewarded with a special bed, at that very moment under construction – 'seven and a half feet long, my son, and made of teak throughout' – there was nothing in the world on which I could possibly wish to spend money. 'You will be able to save, my son,' he said, concluding his discourse on the generous arrangement he was so soon to end.

I put my Diplomas away in a drawer and never looked at them again. My father went back to England. Mother and I were left alone in the house, with one all-round servant, Mary Farrell, a cleaning woman 'off the place', Mrs Doolan, and Michael Barratt, the so-called houseboy who became and remained an indispensable part of everyone's life.

Within a week I had written to the Mother Superior of the Mater Hospital in Dublin. I would produce for the hospital, I wrote, and for the first time in Ireland, 'Grade A Certified Milk'. For the first time in its history, I wrote, Ireland would have a hospital in which no patient would be exposed to milk-borne diseases. A new day was dawning for Ireland, and a letter from her would set in motion an agricultural revolution fit to rank with that begun by Count Plunkett, A. E. Russell and my father – the Creamery Movement. A month later I received her reply. 'The Mother Superior of the Mater Hospital, Dublin, is perfectly satisfied with the hospital's present milk supplier.'

My father had once again bought me a motor car – the black Ford had mercifully vanished once again – a second-hand wire-wheeled Peugeot of extremely ancient vintage. It was a dangerous and badly knocked about ruin, but I loved it dearly. It was the only serious motor car for miles around but there was nearly always something wrong with it. The tyres were worn to shreds when it arrived. My father – of course in order to save money – had bought it in London and shipped it at great expense to Waterford. There I had to go by wearisome train, and the car broke down three times on the way home. The old-fashioned magneto was only inches from the ground and one drop of water splashed up from the merest puddle meant hours of delay, the partial dismemberment of the engine, and an eternity of drying and polishing by handkerchief before any hope of starting again. Sometimes I waited for hours beside that greatly loved vehicle for another motorist to pass who would deliver a message to a garage. But there were few motorists and fewer garages in Tipperary in 1924. Several times I spent all night on the road.

One day I set off for Limerick with a new plan for revolutionising the butter-making industry of Ireland. Some of the great creameries of the Golden Vale had already amalgamated and I was to lunch with the Group Chairman. He spoke with warm affection of my father and he was wonderful over lunch. Ireland was indeed a lucky country to have so fine a son of so grand a father returning to modernise the land. What the country needed was more young men like me, young men of learning and initiative, innovators, go-getters, men seeing the real future of Ireland laid out clearly as on a map of the mind. It was the greatest of pities, he said, pouring another glass of wine, that movement forward had to be so slow, that he had to carry six hundred farmers and a very sticky committee along with him towards that beautiful dawn I was predicting. Of course it would come, but there was, alas, nothing he could do to hurry the process: 'D'ye know what,' he said, 'there does be difficulties besetting all of us these days.' The car went badly on the long road home.

Every day I walked, and sometimes rode on Brownie, over

Synone, all 987 acres of it. We employed twenty-three men and Jack Heffernan rang the bell for them every morning at seven as he had rung it five years earlier, in 'Mrs Nicolson's time'. Round about Christmas the men decided to strike for better pay and conditions. I thought they needed those myself, but my father saw his Irish employees as he saw his youngest son, plutocrats all, living in ease and comfort, with no worries about the fluctuations in the cotton market, the anxieties of owning and running factories in Ealing, warehouses in Smithfield, vast quantities of worthless shares, twenty or thirty houses, and all on a frugal habit of life. But of course there must be no strike; his youngest son must see to that.

On a bleak evening Jack Heffernan came over to the house. The men were in the yard coach-house, 'not satisfied to work'. I picked up the balance sheets, was smiled at by my mother, and walked across to the yard. There they all were, having just refused to take their Friday wages. They gave me a cheerful concerted 'Good evening' and pushed forward a reluctant Jim Ryan (who afterwards married Mary Farrell), to speak for them. He was a magnificent hurler, playing for Boherlahan and the County, but not much of a spokesman. All the same I found myself in general agreement with him. When he'd finished Jack held up a storm lantern and I showed them the balance sheets and told them, with the proofs of what I was saying, that we had lost over twenty-five thousand pounds since my father had bought Synone. 'Let's not stand here, messing about,' I said and I proposed an immediate settlement. It wouldn't break us to give them another half crown a week and they should, as I thought they deserved, have that right away. I told them that we would no longer deduct a shilling a week for ploughing and renting to each man a quarter of an Irish acre of potato ground. I had to plough our own, I said, and I might as well go on for another day or two and plough theirs. There would be no future deductions for ass-grazing provided it was *one* ass. They laughed when I told them that on the books less than a dozen asses were shown but that every day as I went round I came across twenty or more. I said I thought it was ridiculous to charge them for a forkful of straw carried home now and again, but that I would still expect a pound if they cut down a permitted tree. They all went home very happy, and although one or

135

two local farmers, and of course my father, grumbled at my 'great generosity' we never had any more labour trouble. Wages just went steadily up as they were doing all over the world. My father lived to see men getting very nearly two pounds a week. Naturally he never thought they earned so enormous a sum.

I became chairman of the Boherlahan Agricultural and Dairying Co-operative Association, known as 'The Creamery'. I had been invited to a committee meeting almost as soon as I arrived home and found myself with my fellow committeemen faced with a major problem, gigantic, insoluble. What were we to do about the chairmanship? The parish priest was chairman and he could not be removed but he had never once attended a meeting, he was entirely ignorant of the affairs of the Creamery and quite uninterested. What could be done? A parish priest in those days was an enormously powerful figure, nearly always for good, but sometimes, through indolence, ignorance or age, a power not exactly for evil, but for something far from actual good. I seldom met one I liked except Dean Innocent Ryan of Cashel: I loved him. But 'The Canon' down in Boherlahan was a very special case, reserved, old, fond of money, and interested in various quackeries, such as water cures and the pressure hose-piping of rheumatics. How were we to get rid of him? Let us make him Perpetual President,' I said. 'That sounds grand and takes away the hidden dead hand from our proceedings.' No one had thought of that; there was a shout of joy, and I was elected chairman on the spot. There and then I composed a letter to the Canon which was regarded as a work of genius. It was a step towards the rat trap; it was part of the writing on the wall.

When the excitements of that first evening were over we all walked across the road to the general store and pub kept by Mr Maher, the schoolmaster, a nice man with two lovely daughters, ripe for dalliance. As we drank our Guinness, a small local farmer said: 'Did the father ever tell you how I stuck him up in the Troubles and took fifty pounds off him?'

'It was you, was it?' I said. 'Yes; he often told me of masked men bursting in on him at pistol point.'

'It was a good night,' the farmer said. 'Mind you, a couple of the lads were a bit trigger-happy in those days and they sent me to make sure the father was quite safe; we were in Limerick by daybreak.'

I wrote and told my father about that but he was never greatly amused at things which appealed to me.

There was the great Sugar Beet Plan. There is now a sugar beet factory in Thurles but there wasn't then and a big meeting was held to canvass for the building of one. Every farmer who attended came to guarantee an acreage and there was a sensation when, after this man and that had risen to promise five, three or two acres, I got up and said, 'My father guarantees fifty Irish acres.' The factory went to Carlow all the same, and there wasn't one in Thurles until years after I had left Ireland. We grew ten acres for Carlow each year and hard labour it was, pulling up the beets, twisting off the tops for ensilage, carting them out to hard roads, where lorries would pick them up, waiting for the money. It was a long, slow, not very profitable business. Everyone hated it, but it was a cash crop and that was something.

At one of these meetings I witnessed an Irish tax collector at work. I think that in the early days of the Free State the tax gatherers worked on commission, like St Matthew, but I could be wrong. Half a dozen of us were sitting in Hayes Hotel drinking, laughing, chatting about the hard labour of farming when a servant came in. Would Mr Billy O'Ryan step out for a moment? There was 'a man asking for you, sir, in the hall beyant'. I have made up his name; it doesn't matter. Billy stepped out. I heard voices, one of them rising to shouts. Then there were screams. No one moved, no one said anything. Billy rejoined us, his false teeth all smashed in his hand, his face running blood. He was crying. I suppose he'd forgotten to pay, or delayed a bit. We didn't ask him. We went on talking and after a few minutes went into the beet meeting.

I'd go to a race meeting now and again, but they usually bored me to distraction. The walking round and round of overtrained underfed screws, thin as a gate, all entered in £150 selling plates; the captains and majors of the First War strolling about sneering; the occasional 'gentleman' knowing no one, graciously nodding his way round and about; the rat-faced jockeys, the smell of corruption. But I did once enjoy a race meeting. My mother one morning asked me to do her a special favour. Would I 'run into Cashel and get me a loaf, dear. We're right out of bread, Mary says.' I got into my little Peugeot and set off. I got the loaf and went down to the post office to see if there were any letters. On the steps stood a beautiful young woman. 'You'll be taking me to the Junction, will you not, Kevin?' she said. She meant the race meeting at Limerick Junction forty miles away. Of course I would. 'Give me a minute for the bank,' I said, 'and I'm your man.'

I now had no salary at all but 'power to draw money'. I drew some blunt from my father's account and we set off. The beautiful lady's father was a famous trainer of racehorses and naturally she was penniless. We entered the enclosure and began to lay our bets. I soon found I was betting for my companion's sister as well as for her and myself. From time to time a race took place, when a few broken-down weeds would amble round the course, some of them too ill to get over the first few jumps. But all afternoon nothing passed the post first while carrying my money, that of my companion, or that of her sister. From time to time the auctioneer for the selling races – who was later to marry my sister Carrie – would give his tremendous laugh and dig me in the ribs. 'You have a nice bit of the real stuff with you there, Kevin,' he'd say.

It was all fun but I was down about twenty pounds of 1924 money as we made for the pretty lady's home. It was full of people drinking. Every house around a racecourse in Ireland – and that means within thirty miles of a racecourse – is always full of people drinking when the meeting ends. After a while the pretty lady said: 'You're taking me to the dance, Kevin?' 'Of course I am,' I said, 'but alas, I'm in the wrong clothes, so I can't.' 'Ah, clothes,' she said in that Irish way which keeps breaking people's hearts. 'Not a soul but'll be in the breeches and boots like yourself.' So I took her to the dance. At seven o'clock the next morning I walked into my mother's bedroom. 'Here's your loaf, Mother,' I said.

It's a poor country dance in Ireland which stops before it's light enough to see the way home. What a pretty creature she was, dancing the night away with a young man pledged elsewhere!

The dance in Mallow was a different affair. The Irish Ministry of Agriculture kept pressing us to grade up our milking herd and help the neighbourhood by keeping one of their Dairy Shorthorn bulls. This was a trouble to work in with the Aberdeen Angus, but it could be managed and it was managed. But it meant that I had to join the Irish Dairy Shorthorn Breeders Association and that year they held their annual meeting in Mallow. Off I went to Cork with an overnight case, all breeches and top boots, and a pocket full of my father's money. I put up at 'The Hotel', which in Ireland means the only 'half-decent' place where you could spend the night. At the meeting there was a man with an amusing face who spoke to me; his name was Michael Buckley. He was a technical representative for a body called the British Sulphate of Ammonia Federation (BSAF). 'There's a bit of a dance after this,' he said, 'just a country hop for small farmers and the like; you'll look in on us, I'm sure.' I didn't know him then, as I was later to know him, and I merely asked about my clothes. 'You'll be overdressed,' he said. 'Most of the bosthoons will be in old tweed trousers and boots; sure most of them'll come on after the evening milking.' I went back to 'The Hotel', washed, had supper, and drove off to the dance. All the women were in full evening dress, every man, including Michael Buckley, in white tie and tails. All the same, I had the night of my life. For the last three hours I clumped round the room with a girl in green – I never knew her name – and at six o'clock I drove her thirty miles home. I thought I'd get to bed after all that but I was wrong. The proprietress of 'The Hotel' had a keen Cork eye to business. The sharpest eye in the world is a Cork eye if there is any money in sight. Her client safely off to the dance for the night, she had promptly let the room to another man. He wouldn't get up and he wouldn't open the door. I slept on a chair, ate a huge breakfast, paid my bill, and left. It took me ten hours to get home, finishing on a tow rope to Cashel and being driven the last five miles by 'Joe' from Hannigans, dug out of his bed for the purpose. My little car was beginning to cost my father a lot of money.

It was because of my pig that I had no money of my own. As soon as I had settled in after coming from Kilmarnock, Mr Willington made me a present of the best young sow in his famous herd of Large Whites. As we took her out of her crate and settled her for the night I could see a long line of red first prize cards decorating her wall. I told my father she was a great beauty and would become famous. 'She'll become an income,' my father said. 'Now that you have stock of your own, my son, you need no salary from me.' He never paid me again, but arranged for me to draw cheques on the farm account in his name. As I had no other money, the farm paid for me from that day onwards. I began to live as I have always lived, a very poor man rubbing a worn shoulder against very rich people. You get used to it quite soon. After twenty or thirty years you hardly notice it.

There was a private creamery in Cashel, the Rose Bower, owned and run by a Northern Irishman, McClusky, and his sister. They were business friends of my father's and both became personal friends of mine. One day, sitting in McClusky's office, I said I thought Cashel needed an agricultural show. And somehow, inevitably, inexorably, one thing led to another until the first meeting of what became the Cashel Agricultural Show Committee. I was elected to the chair. Then we elected McClusky secretary. Willie Ryan of 'The Hotel' said that he thought that 'a kind of a class of a horse show' would be desirable. Someone asked: 'What about the odd cow, now, or maybe a pig?' Jack Heffernan thought that we 'might have a kind of little general show'.

We began to talk about money and the testing of public opinion; the fair of Cashel was the following Tuesday, we would walk up and down, chatting up farmers, seeing if they would contribute, if they would actually promise to show a horse or cow or pig. We separated in a state of interested excitement.

On Tuesday Jack Heffernan and I walked the fair together. We began outside Corcoran's Hotel and we finished outside Willie Ryan's. By then we had fifty pounds in our pockets and as many promises of exhibits. Over a few drinks we found that other members of the committee had done as well, visiting bars, going in and out of shops, and calling on Monsignor Innocent Ryan, Dean of Cashel. He had wished our project well, blessed us as 'kindly thoughtful men, with the love of Ireland in our hearts', and Cashel Show was in the bag.

All through the winter and early spring of 1924/5 we called on farmers, we wrote to them, we cadged money from any who seemed remotely cadgeable. We advertised. Donations poured in, cups and medals were offered for competition; we began to get letters from all over Ireland.

We raised our sights. We would have horse jumping competitions and a grandstand, we would have a judging ring. This was going to be no hole and corner affair in a field; this was to be the biggest one-day show ever held in Ireland. We set up local classes, small farmer classes, all-Ireland open classes. If a man was known to have a good pig, he got a letter; if he had a nice herd of pedigree cattle or a flock of sheep, one of us called. By early spring our prize list was ready and we printed 2,000 copies of it. The size and quality of the entries was surprising and a month before the show date we had entries from every one of the thirty-two counties of Ireland, including the six 'across the border'. One year later that prize list ruined us.

We began to construct our showground. I gave the timber for the Grand Ring and two farming brothers gave the grandstand timber. We allotted the catering rights, and we laid out a jumping course. The double bank, an essential part of all Irish jumping competitions, took us a month to build. We had a huge water jump, a single bank, and a fairly stiff stone wall. It was a good course and we received a big jumping entry. I gave a cup for a pair of fat bullocks and another for the best dairy cow in the parish of Boherlahan. That was the little time bomb which ticked away towards our ultimate destruction. Ten pounds worth of paper-thin silver, not much larger than a tea cup, and it blew up in our faces.

The show, when the great day arrived, was a gigantic success. It was a glorious day, the hottest of the summer, and the whole countryside poured in on us. By two o'clock in the afternoon it was impossible to buy a drink, either on the showground or anywhere in Cashel, and emergency supplies were speeding towards us from Thurles, Fethard, Cahir, and Clonmel. Someone was discovered selling water at twopence a glass which almost provoked a lynching. That would at least have been an attraction – but it passed off peacefully in the end. I won fourteen first prizes and would have won fifteen but for an act of unaccountable altruism. I was stewarding the pigs and saw my young sow duly win first prize, the judge hardly bothering to look at her, she was so beautiful. But there was a better pig on the ground and I had seen it. The owner was confused by the crowd and still had her in a creel by the entrance gate. I felt I had to take the judge along to look at her, and he at once altered his decision and put me down to second.

But Synone had one truly exciting win. Mick Barratt, with the mare of the plough team behind which I had driven my first furrow, nearly five years earlier, stormed up the short grass hill in the weight-pulling competition with nearly thirty-five hundredweight of iron in the competition tip-cart. He was an almost perfect horseman, was Mick; he never touched the mare, just spoke to her as she reached the slope, and fifteen paces later he had the red rosette.

It was six o'clock when Fate struck. We'd survived some tremendous upheavals during the day – the row over the Dean's Mass on the showyard at eight a.m., the non-lynching of the water seller, and the false particulars given by someone who had bought one of our own Suffolk rams and now exhibited it as several months younger than I knew it was. He claimed he couldn't see that a few months made 'ere a difference'. But at six o'clock there came into McClusky's office a small quiet farmer from Boherlahan to collect his cup for 'the best cow in the parish'. This was Mike McTigue of Tubberadora – Fate in person. He smiled the happy smile of a clear winner and said to McClusky: 'I've come for me cup, sir.' McClusky smiled back. His name was Tom but he was the only man for miles around whom nobody called by his Christian name. He was greatly respected, was that fiery man from Antrim. 'And never was a cup better earned and won, Mike,' he said, getting the cup out of the cupboard in his office and fondling it. 'She's young and beautiful, that cow of yours and she'll win out the cup for you. Just sign this receipt and you can go home a happy man.'

'I have the cup won, Mr McClusky,' said Mike.

'You have indeed; twice more and it's yours,' said McClusky.

'I have the cup won; it's my cup,' said Mike.

Good tempers were still prevailing, no one was yet disturbed. I was tired and happy and lolling back in the office chair. McClusky stood, running his hands over my little cup. He put it down on the table and picked up our show catalogue then opened the catalogue and read from it: 'Cup, presented by Mr Kevin FitzGerald of Synone for the best cow in milk in the parish of Boherlahan, to be won three times, not necessarily in succession, before becoming the property of the winner. There you are, Mike,' he said cheerfully, 'sign this receipt and off with you now with the prize money and cup.'

'I have the cup won,' said Mike. He pulled out our prize list which we had put out so many months ago, long before the catalogue, and opened it at the page he wanted. He read out: 'Cup presented by Mr Kevin FitzGerald of Synone for the best cow in milk in the parish of Boherlahan.' ''Tis an outright win I have,' he said. 'Give me the cup, Mr McClusky.'

'I mustn't interfere in this,' I said, and slipped out of the office. I was wrong. I should have stayed. I should have given Mike the cup. I should have given him two cups, or even three.

It was not till a few days later that I heard how the row developed. That night there was the all-night show dance, at which 'Valentia' was played sixteen times and a man from Cahir went home because I had two dances with his girl. Ireland is no safe place to have two dances with anyone's girl. It was not long since there had been a cross-country chase in high-powered motor cars, pursued and pursuer firing at each other with revolvers brought home from the war. That too was because of a nice girl who had two dances with someone else. I got home from the show dance at half past eight in the morning and I wasn't thinking about Mike McTigue.

But Mike had stuck to it that the cup was his and McClusky had lost his temper. After a while what is called in Ireland 'The Hard Word' was spoken, the cup had been dramatically thrust back into its cupboard, and Mike, 'wearing the black look', had gone home.

We had a committee meeting or two, the days passed from drought into the normal summer rains of central Ireland, my father, who had come over for the show and greatly enjoyed it, lingered on, to the delight of my mother and the horror of everyone else, and we began to think about harvest and the winter.

One autumn day a Civic Guard came out from Cashel and asked for me. 'I have to put this in your very own hand, sir', he said. It was a summons, calling upon Thomas McClusky, creamery owner, and Kevin FitzGerald, gentleman, to show cause why they were withholding a silver cup presented by the aforesaid Kevin FitzGerald, gentleman, for the best cow in the parish, from Mr Mike McTigue of Tubberadora. I thanked the Guard, got out my motor car and drove over to the Rose Bower Creamery.

McClusky was raging. We'd do this, we'd do that, we'd see poor Mike McTigue in hell. I said we'd go and see a solicitor and we did. He told us we hadn't a leg to stand on and McClusky shouted that he wanted counsel's opinion. The very man we wanted was at that moment defending a case in Clonmel, our solicitor said, and if we rushed over we'd get him when he came out of court. I drove McClusky over to Clonmel and we saw the great man in his private rooms in 'The Hotel', drinking a bottle of claret and eating a couple of chops. He read the summons, read the prize list, read the catalogue. 'You haven't a hope in hell,' he said, 'give the bloody man the cup'. 'If I drop dead, he could have it,' said McClusky, 'if not, not.' 'All right,' said the counsel, 'we'll give it a run, but you'll lose. But don't mind that, I'll cost you nothing, I'll donate my fee to the funds of the Society.'

We trusted that barrister that darkling autumn evening. We were young, we were silly. We came away fairly happy.

The case was to come on, we learned, as the weeks dragged by, towards the end of the year. In the meantime there was the row with the Dean to be settled, with the parish of Cashel beginning to split down the middle.

It seemed that when the Dean arrived to say the Mass for the opening of the show, he had been ill received. No one was there to bid him good-day; McClusky had rushed into the Creamery office where the Dean was vesting, calling out 'Hurry up, Dean, we've a busy day before us', and Willie Ryan of 'The Hotel', knowing nothing of that, had walked in with 'You're nice and late this morning, Dean, and all the Barony awake since five.' The Dean had begun to leave, had been persuaded to stay and say the Mass by some local saint, but had gone off without a word afterwards and had not attended the show.

There were those who held that both McClusky and Willie Ryan were walking about in a state of mortal sin and should be excommunicated. McClusky had called to make his peace but the Dean had made some thoughtless remark and McClusky had flounced out and written a note. I saw a copy of it. It ended 'slamming your own door on my back and shaking every window in John Street'. Much fat was in the fire, and I went to see the Dean.

Going to see the Dean was always a great occasion. I would knock at the door and Mary, the Dean's housekeeper, would open it. The Dean would advance upon me and take both my hands. 'Mary,' he always said, 'bring in the Black Bottle.' '*Not* the Black Bottle, Dean,' Mary would say firmly, 'just the Visitors' Bottle.' 'You heard me, Mary,' the Dean would say. 'Get the Black Bottle.' ''Tis just as you say, Dean; if the Black Bottle is wanted then it must be brought'; and Mary would depart to get it, with just the slightest suggestion of a flounce.

The Black Bottle was a treat indeed. The Dean had a supply of something which he hoped would last out his life. He never touched the contents himself or any drink. But the Black Bottle was for Archbishops, Presidents, and one or two of the Dean's personal friends. I had that great honour and privilege. The Black Bottle was filled from a keg of potheen which had been made a hundred years back and which had lain buried in a Mayo bog for eighty. It was colourless and the first sip had to be taken neat. At once the finger tips were conscious of it, accompanied by a mental feeling that all the troubles of the world had been healed. After that the least drip of water could be added, a lovely soft glow filled the room, the Dean began to speak in the voice of an angel, and time stood still. The Black Bottle was an experience – quite enough for one long well-spent life time – and here I was seeing that Bottle and sipping its contents for the third time, at the age of twenty-three.

'Dean,' I said, 'let me bring Tom McClusky and Willie Ryan here.'

That tremendous man took out his handkerchief and wiped his eyes.

'Oh, my dear friend,' he said, 'my dear, dear friend, I'm supposed to look after the flock, to guard them and love them. All I did was to lose my temper and shout. What sort of conduct is that at all, at all?'

'I have them in Cullen's Bar at the bottom of the street, Dean,' I said.

'Ah Kevin,' he said, 'run.'

I went out of the house, and hurried the hundred yards to

Cullen's, to fetch the two culprits. The Dean was standing on his doorstep with tears pouring down his face. You often read that; you don't often see it. His arms were stretched wide and he put them round Tom McClusky. 'Tom,' he said, 'if we hadn't Kevin where would we be?' Willie Ryan held out his withered arm, and smiled. 'Dean,' he said, 'me head is ready for the hatchet.' They stood shaking hands and clinging to each other until the Dean asked them in for a drink. Mary had been quick and the Black Bottle had gone. She appeared in the doorway of the Dean's study with the Visitors' Bottle and glasses. I had drunk of ambrosia and refused any other drink. I said goodnight to the Dean, grinned at my friends, and walked out to my little motor car. With the wonderful Black Bottle continuing its miracle, I sang loudly and happily all the way back to Synone.

The case of Mike McTigue of Tubberadora versus Thomas McClusky, creamery proprietor, and Kevin FitzGerald, gentleman, was still ticking away. At last it came on in the Old Court House, Tipperary Town, about a month before Christmas. I was not to be called as a witness and I drove over to Tipperary only just in time to get a seat. About two hundred people had taken a day off to see the fun. I went into the barristers' robing room to have a final chat with McClusky and to say 'Hallo' to Mike's counsel. He shook hands with me, saying, 'You haven't a dog's chance today, but it's all great fun, and my fee is going to your Society.'

I went back to the body of the court and made the great blunder of the day. Mike came in, surrounded by his supporters. He looked uncertainly at me and I got up and shook hands with him. He was after all my neighbour. 'Nice to see you,' I said, 'I hope we all have a good day.' As I sat down John Heffernan, who of course had come with me, whispered: 'Ah God, Master Kevin, you have us all destroyed; you should have turned away the head as he looked towards you.' 'Rubbish,' I said, 'he's only just brought back the sugarbeet forks we lent him. This is a friendly action.' 'Ah, friendly,' he said and lapsed into frowning silence.

The judge took his seat, the clerk called our case, counsel opened with a fair and reasonably light-hearted account of the general situation and McClusky was called to give evidence.

All counsel, I suppose – and all Irish counsel I well know – try to make a witness lose his temper. Mike's counsel had no trouble at all with McClusky. Within minutes he was, as Jack Heffernan whispered in my ear, 'raving'. At one point Mike's counsel asked him: 'You would agree, Mr McClusky, that your prize list offered the cup unconditionally?' 'And bloody well that schamer knew the rights of it,' was the answer. 'You mustn't swear like that in my court, Mr McClusky,' said the judge. 'Indeed and I'm sorry your Honour, but he's bloody well driving me up the wall, picking on me, and bloody well he knows it.'

The judge, a real nice man, smiled at him. 'Now just calm down, Mr McClusky,' he said. 'If ever there was a case for amicable settlement, this case is it. I'm going to adjourn for a quarter of an hour while you do just that.' He got up and left the court. I went out into the yard with McClusky, Mike and the two counsel. A 'ring' had already been formed, as if for a prize fight under the old bare knuckle rules. I found myself inside the ring with our opponents. Mike's counsel spoke first: 'Come on now, Mr McClusky. All you have to do is to give my client, a decent honest man, the cup he has well and truly earned and we can all go home.' 'Is it go home,' said McClusky, 'leaving our cup in the hands of that bloody twister?' I told McClusky to shut up, that he would have us all in quod for libel. 'What do you want us to do?' I asked Mike. 'Only give me me cup, sir,' he said.

You read about people going purple and looking as though about to have a fit, I've only seen it once in my life and it was then. McClusky did not actually foam but he did go a deep purple colour and I really thought he might have some kind of seizure. When he could speak, he said: 'Dear and Holy God,' he said, 'is it only give me me cup and let me home he wants? Is it keep for his bloody self the cup that himself and every decent man for miles around knows was given by Mr FitzGerald here to be won three times?' He glared at Mike's counsel. 'He knows it, I tell you, he knows it.'

'Maybe he does, McClusky,' said the counsel, 'and maybe he doesn't, but your prize list, and never mind your catalogue, says it's his cup. You offered it for the best cow in the parish, he has the best cow in the parish, he brought it to your show, the judge awarded him the cup, and he wants it in Tubberadora. Come on now, Mr McClusky, give him his cup and let's all have a bit of peace.'

'And what do you say?' McClusky asked our counsel. 'I fear me learned friend is right,' he said. 'I recommend that you give him the cup now, and that we all go across the road for a half one.'

'I'd rather die this minute,' said McClusky, and we all went back into the court.

Mike gave his evidence and it was a lot better given than McClusky's. Mike assumed the role of the simple, rather poor and bewildered small farmer. And he did it well. Our counsel couldn't shift him. When he'd seen the prize list he'd thought he had a chance of winning Mr FitzGerald's cup. He had the cow for it, and he'd entered her. He'd given her 'the least bit of a little wash, a child, mind you, could walk her about, and she on the place from a calf, and the show judge had liked her, as who wouldn't, and had given her first prize, and the cup. You'd only to see her to know that in Dublin itself she couldn't be beat.'

The judge was getting fed up with all this, 'Gentlemen,' he said, 'we could be all day about this. It's getting on for lunch time and I'm adjourning this case again for ten minutes. Come back then and tell me you've settled. You all know what to do, but just in case you don't I'll give you the least hint. This little cup could be re-presented, couldn't it?' He went back to his room.

We went once more into the re-formed ring. 'Well now,' said our counsel to his learned friend, 'what about it?' Mike's counsel knew just what the judge had in mind, so did I, so did McClusky, so did everyone in the ring. 'Give Mr McTigue his cup,' he said, 'and he'll give it straight back to the Society.' He looked at his client. 'You'll do that?' 'I will, of course,' said Mike. 'All I want is the rags of me honour saved and proclaimed in an open court, as it might be this one, this very day.' 'Well, what about that?' asked our counsel. McClusky couldn't speak and I answered for us both. 'Yes of course,' I said, 'we'll gladly give him the cup if he is going to give it back to us.' 'Let Mr McClusky and my client shake hands on that,' said Mike's counsel.

McClusky found some sort of voice although his own sister (he had no wife) wouldn't have recognised it. 'And am I to add to total humiliation the clutching hand of a lizard?' he shouted. 'Ah, shake hands like men,' shouted someone at the back of the ring, and the cry was taken up. It was like the closing moments of a cattle deal at a fair. 'Let two decent honest men shake hands,' cried voices from everywhere. 'I'll make a start,' I said to our counsel. I put out my hand to Mike. 'Come on now, Mike,' I said. 'Do I get me cup, Master Kevin?' he asked me. 'You do,' I said, 'on the terms we've been talking about, and His Honour wants.' 'Fair enough, sir,' he said and we shook. We had arrived at what climbers call 'the crux', the hard move of the day. I've said that no one ever called McClusky by his Christian name, but I did now. 'Shake his hand, Tom,' I said. The atmosphere had changed, the whole crowd was silent. Then McClusky spoke, quietly, choosing every word. 'If death came to me this moment,' he said, 'it would come as a blessing, for I would be spared the horror of hearing it suggested that I take the hand of a hound.'

It was Mike's turn to say his piece: 'And little thought I, saying my bits of morning prayer, and rising up from my bed this day, that ere noon I would be asked to take the hand of a man notorious throughout the Barony for watering the very buttermilk from which the last drop of crame has been squeezed. Buttermilk from that creamery wouldn't put flesh on a rat, never mind a pig, and it starving.'

Both men clenched their fists and it was clear that either hands must be shaken or blows exchanged. 'Come on the pair of you,' I said, 'shake hands and let's get back into court and then let's all have a drink.'

No one moved in the whole crowd except the two men. They turned their backs on each other and each man stuck out his right hand behind him. I guided those hands into position myself. As they met, McClusky said, as he knew he must: 'That the cup may be lucky with you,' and Mike said, as he knew he must: 'That the settlement may be lucky with you.' We all pushed our way back into court. Each counsel began whispering into the ear of his client and the judge came back.

Mike's counsel announced a settlement, the judge beamed, and McClusky, prompted by our counsel, rose and spoke. The words came slowly, but he got them out. So far from being purple he was now a yellowish-white colour and his hands

149

shook. He was a fine handsome middle-aged man but at that moment he could have been taken for ninety. 'As Secretary of the Cashel Agricultural Show Society,' he said, 'I now hand to Mr Michael McTigue of Tubberadora the cup presented by Mr Kevin FitzGerald of Synone for the best cow in the parish, which he has won outright, and which remains his property.'

I had not known that my poor little ten-pound cup was in court but McClusky reached under his chair and produced it. Mike rose in his place. He too had quickly learned his part. 'I, Michael McTigue of Tubberadora in the parish of Boherlahan, accept the cup which I have won outright for possessing the best cow in the parish, and I hereby present it to the Cashel Agricultural Show Society to be competed for annually in a class for the best cow in the parish, the cup to be won three times, not necessarily in succession, before becoming the property of the exhibitor.' He sat down in a gale of laughter which the judge led.

'That's a fine cow you must have, Mr McTigue, to have all this great fuss made of her. Is it gold dust you feed her on?' 'Ah, no, your Honour,' said Mike, 'just a lock of hay when I have it, a bit of oat straw, a turnip now and then. She's as poor as meself, your Honour, but richer in summer. She can eat the grass, she can – but I must still go hungry, and herself and the childher.' Mike was an artist. There was a lot more laughter, the judge made the necessary orders, and we all went home. I thought it was all over, but it was only just beginning.

Of course we had to pay the costs. Our counsel's fee was enormous and there was no longer any suggestion that the Society would have it. Our solicitors' charges would have bought a couple of pedigree heifers. Mike McTigue's counsel took the fee which he too had said would be coming to us and his solicitors' charges would have taken a duke to the Riviera. We might have survived all that but the heart had gone out of us and I suppose it showed. Word must have gone round that we'd taken a knock and that there wasn't too much in the bank.

Bills and claims for expenses began to pour in on us. The brothers who had given the timber for the grandstand sent in a demand for £200. All kinds of volunteers discovered that we owed them for labour, motor-car and horse-trap journeys, visits to printers, standing rounds of drinks. Several unworthy shop-keepers, none of them from Cashel, sent in bills for exhibiting show posters, and when all was done and paid we were over £400 in debt. Only a month or two earlier we had been sitting on a profit of £1,000 and more, and were eagerly looking forward to the following year and another tremendous show. That dream was over. We sold our grandstand for its timber, we sold the judging ring, we sold all the timber we had put up for horse and cattle lines and stalls. When we had finished paying out and were just clear, all that was left of the Cashel Agricultural Show Society were the concrete remains of our great turfed double bank, a silent monument to what might have been. I've often wondered what happened to my cup for the best cow in the parish. It was never mentioned again.

The winter of 1925/6 was a good winter for us, with everything going reasonably well. The Suffolk ram lamb sales had been a disappointment – we had still to become known as breeders – but we had some very good young bulls coming on for the annual bull show in Dublin. Of one of these, in particular, I was very proud. As a tiny calf he developed 'white scour', a genuine killer, usually owing to dirt. I told my mother we could save the calf if we cut our sleep for a couple of nights and we decided to try. Every two hours for those two days and nights, my mother heated milk and I added brandy to it, walked over to the yard, fed the calf. I suppose he was paralytically drunk all the time but on the third morning he stood up, and Mother and I went to our beds for the day. He remained a tiny little animal, but beautiful, and with a fine pedigree. I knew someone would buy him.

Looking after young bulls who are going to be sold for breeding is hard work but fascinating. They must be prepared for showing and handling, they must glow with health, they must be well fleshed without fat. They must be trained to walk calmly and quietly in a halter. A young bull being trained to walk is very strong and he doesn't want to be trained. He knows you are not afraid of him because he will have knocked you down a couple of times in his loose box and you are still coming in with his meals, sometimes, too, coming with two or three men to press him up against the wall as you daub him with sulphur wash to keep his skin from itching so that he won't rub bald patches into his hide. He has to learn to keep his hair on in more senses than one.

When he first walks out he is going to try and run for it. A long rope halter is needed and there are no circumstances in which you may let go. If he is old enough and strong enough he is almost bound to pull you over but you will be doing all this preliminary stuff in a big field and can afford to be dragged along the ground until he is tired of it. If you once let him go, you are never going to teach him; he has the measure of you. After a while he will go for long walks with you on hard ground in a short halter. Gradually you teach him to put out each foot strongly and firmly as if he meant it, to hold up his head and try and catch the judge's eye. There is a hard day's work every day of the week if you and your herdsman have half a dozen bulls in preparation. The herdsman of course will pocket any prize money you win, but to 'get a card' is the reward for everything.

We got through the winter well and in March I won fourth prize in Dublin with a yearling bull in a class of just over forty. My little sick bull won no prize but he took the eye of a small farmer who gave a good price for him. Two years later he had sired a Dublin winner, but I was not there to see it.

At the spring show I got a Very Highly Commended card with a ram, and a private commendation from the judge. He would have given me second prize, he said, if I hadn't shown my ram with a tiny embryo horn. 'You should have taken it out,' he said. 'But that's specifically forbidden in the Society's rules,' I told him.

'My son,' he said, 'look along these stalls. Every winner there has had an embryo horn taken out of his head, and I'll lay you a shade of odds that most of the lamb winners were born at least two months before Christmas.' 'I suppose they were,' I said, 'mine was born on January 2nd.' He gave me a pitying look. 'Of course it was,' he said, and left me.

In the early summer, just into May, my father arrived for a visit. I met him at Gooldscross and drove him home. Because of his visit and for no other reason, we had had two men out with horse-drawn thistle cutters for the past five weeks but we had wasted our effort. 'Thistles everywhere, I see,' said my father as we came up the avenue. 'There is an air of dilapidation about everything which appals me. Has nothing been done on this place since my last visit, is it all "Go day, come day, God send Sunday" as it has been with you all too often?' I told him that we had been rather busy, of the hundred bullocks tied up all winter and only just sold, of the thirty heifers, now gone the way of all flesh, of the hard time with the lambing only just over, of the rains delaying the preparation of good seed beds, of much more. We were in the house by this time and he began raging about the state of the garden. Mother asked him to get settled before he went on any more and he calmed down.

That long early summer visit was a time of dread for those compelled to experience it. Every day, in his vast panama hat, his thick malacca cane in hand, our unmanageable Airedale 'Bob' bounding around him, my father would set forth on 'a walk round the place'. Invariably he returned with a list of complaints. I would hear of thistles everywhere (they were to the end of his life the King Charles's Head of my father), cattle looking miserable and neglected, wretched beasts, heavily in calf; sheep 'limping painfully, my son', ruin staring at him in every field. 'There is a gate in Farranavarra crying out for attention. I do not speak of these things, my son, but I notice them.' I think he really believed that he never spoke of these things.

The breaking point was reached just after mid-May. Mother had gone to bed and my father and I sat over the essential all-the-year-round fire of the drawing room. He was bland. After a while and some chit-chat he remarked: 'I think, my son, that later in the summer you should attend the great sheep fair in Ballinasloe and purchase two hundred Galway ewes.' He liked the sound of the words 'Galway ewes', and repeated them. My father never though in tens or even dozens. Two hundred was for him a nice round figure. He had enjoyed arranging a bank credit for me in Ballinasloe when I bought just that number of ewes the preceding late summer. 'Another two hundred Galway ewes,' he said again.

'We've too many sheep on the place as it is,' I said, 'the herds are bringing in a dead one most days. In Johnston's time there was sheep sickness here, and I wouldn't be all that sure that we're far from it just now.'

My father had the trick of drawing slowly on his cigar as if drawing it *at* someone. He did that now. 'There are matters you do not understand, do not entirely comprehend, my son. The fluctuation of markets, the rise and fall of prices, the economics of rural life, of which you enjoy the fruits, are perhaps beyond you. Mr Johnston ran two thousand sheep on this place, your books show a mere twelve hundred.'

I said: 'Johnston wasn't milking thirty-five cows, grazing the best part of two hundred cattle, about to try and fatten fifty of them on the grass down in Farranavarra.'

'The Golden Hoof of the sheep enriches the owner,' said my father. 'Listen, Dad,' I said. 'We have at this moment, on this place now, while I'm talking, two hundred ewes suckling their lambs, a hundred 'culled' ewes which we must fatten and sell pretty damn soon, your Suffolk flock and all their lambs which eat just as much as the others, and over two hundred shearlings from which to build up the breeding flock. We've two years wool in the lofts which we can't give away, and you want to add two hundred breeding ewes which, by this time next year, will with their lambs have added the best part of five hundred mouths to the present lot. It can't be done.'

'Ignorance, to which stupidity and obstinacy are added, is a pitiful thing,' said my father. 'When to that is added the touch of arrogance you are at present displaying, an ugly sight appears.'

'You wouldn't think you were perhaps talking about yourself?' I said, picking up the poker. My father leaned down and took up the shovel. Two civilised gladiators, one without a chance, sat facing each other.

'You are not fitted for much,' said my father, 'you take well to a life of idleness and luxury. I imagine a man like you on the prairies of, let us say, Western Canada would starve to death in a week.' My father twirled his shovel and raised his voice. His ordinary speaking voice might have sounded overloud in St Paul's Cathedral. Now it became tremendous, seemed to shake the house. 'You are a very stupid young man, my son,' he said.

I think I began to wave the poker; I know I shouted. 'Not so stupid as a bloody old fool trying to overstock this place,' I bawled. 'I'm off to Canada in the morning, I have had more than enough of you.' The door opened and my mother, in a nightdress and shawl, took the stage. 'Apologise to your father, dear,' she said. 'That's no way for you to talk to him.'

'I'll see him in hell first,' I said, 'I'm off out of here in the morning to starve to death in Canada. A week he gives me.'

My father sat back, smiling, relaxed, smoking peacefully. 'Just say you're sorry, dear,' my mother said, 'then we can all go to bed.'

She was undefeatable. 'I'm sorry, sir,' I said to my father. He smiled at me like a man looking up from a book on hearing that dinner is ready. 'Think nothing of it, my son,' he said. 'A little warmth, the letting off of a little steam, is oftentimes an excellent thing.' He held out his hand and I took it. He had two cardinal virtues as I have said often, and he practised them all the time. He never bore malice, and never imputed unworthy motives to the actions of any man or woman. You really could say of him that if a friend knifed him in the back – and one or two of them were to do just that – he would call it an accident.

In the morning we were all calm. Mother had obviously kept my father awake for most of the night and was strong for my 'going away for a little while'. My father arrived at the breakfast table and moved into details as if we had been planning the whole affair for months. I was to go to London, buy a third-class rail and steamer ticket to Winnipeg, for which he would pay, take ten pounds only, and see what happened. He gave me his big old-fashioned Gladstone bag which I filled with rough clothes and I left for London the following day.

There was a fine show of emotion on my departure, Jack Heffernan's wife in the proper sort of artificial tears, Jack genuinely overcome, Mother calm, my father bidding me a casual goodbye as if I were off to Dublin for the day. I had a great sense of relief as Brownie clip-clopped to Thurles, Jack driving, and silent. He knew as well as I did what it was like to stand up to my father.

My brother William put me up in his City flat for the couple of nights I needed. I spent the whole of my first day at Lord's watching G.T.S. Stephens make a hundred by singles against Armstrong's Australian eleven, devoting the next to making arrangements for my starvation trip to Winnipeg. In 1925 you could buy a ticket for almost anywhere at almost any railway booking office.

155

Seven

My journey to Canada as an immigrant began rather movingly. I was sitting in a packed third-class compartment at Waterloo when a fellow traveller said: 'Someone wants you outside, mate.' I looked up and there was my father. He had followed me from Ireland to see me off, and he was holding a thick pile of envelopes. I got out and stood with him for a few minutes. He feared the worst, he told me, and the envelopes all contained letters of introduction, coast to coast, clear across Canada, beginning with a note to a friend in St John's, Newfoundland, and ending with another on Vancouver Island. I thanked him, he kissed me, and left me stuffing the letters into the top of the old Gladstone bag.

The ship was the *Ascania,* a one-funnel biscuit box of the Cunard Line. She was an appalling old tub and she was going to take ten days to get as far as Quebec. There were four of us to a cabin and we were told by a steward about meals and behaviour. This was an immigrant ship. There was a bar, which sold only beer and soft drinks, there was also a master-at-arms to look after discipline and to prevent night-time excursions after women. There were about two hundred and fifty mixed immigrants, mostly from South Georgia ('Bohunks') or Italy ('Wops'). No one wept on the dockside or even waved as we warped out of Southampton and made for Cherbourg, a very nasty choppy crossing which made half the passengers sick and unhappy.

It was dark when we arrived at Cherbourg and a big tender came off with more foreigners. By that time I was chatting away to a man of my own age who hoped never to see England again. He had already established a pull with the third-class purser and I was exchanged into his cabin with a third occupant we both learned to regret. He unpacked a dinner jacket rather ostentatiously as we joined him and gave us to understand that he was in effect a first-class passenger except that he happened to be in the steerage like us.

I was travelling on a return ticket to Winnipeg, where the prairie began, the prairie on which I was 'to starve inside a week'. My ticket had cost twenty-five pounds all in – but the food was excellent. Throughout our ten-day voyage we had three outsize meals every day, soup at mid-morning, and after-noon tea.

There was trouble once or twice. We had a trifle of fisticuffs now and then. But the master-at-arms and his men were used to all that and kept us pretty quiet on the whole, though the woman problem was more serious. Night after night some Italian or other would be apprehended as he crept along the companionway. There were whole parties of young women kept under lock and key and the eyes of terrifying uniformed matrons. These matrons and the master-at-arms with his staff were kept at full stretch all the way to Quebec and to my knowledge were frequently outwitted.

We formed happy groups as the days went by. I learned to play shuffleboard; I played a little chess; I sat about with various dubious characters. Everyone was oddly cagey about why they were going to Canada and what they were going to do when they got there. Hardly anyone drank anything. I hung on grim-ly to my 'starvation' ten pounds, but had to break into one of them to stand my corner now and then. I was called 'Duke' by all my companions, just as I had been in my old lorry-driving days and I realised quite soon that I was, as always, in the wrong clothes for my new life. I travelled in plus fours, the normal English and Irish country dress of that time. Sometimes a woman I rather liked used to call out 'Here's the Prince of Wales' as I said good morning to her.

I left the ship at Quebec, although my ticket was through to Montreal. My cabin friend, Williams, had to get off there and he was feeling lonely and a bit frightened. Our 'first-class' cabin mate went grandly on, after trying to borrow money from both of us, and actually getting two pounds out of me. I expect he was a success in his new life; he had made a good start. Williams and I seemed to be almost the only two people leaving the ship at Quebec. We were all alone as we were ushered into a vast wire cage for approval and medical examination. I seemed to amuse the doctor enormously. He took Williams more seriously but he was nice to us both, and I was soon on my way to see the

Heights of Abraham. Williams wouldn't come. He was going to walk about, he said, and get the feel of Canada. We agreed to meet on the immigrant train late that afternoon and we did.

In the most mysterious way half the ship was already on it. We had come ashore alone, and I had seen no one other than ourselves in the reception sheds. We at once ganged up with two shipmates for the two-and-a-half days' journey to Winnipeg. We didn't know what it was going to be like, but a look at the train told us most of what was required.

To me the giant locomotive in front was worth the whole trip; her crew, gauntleted and peak-capped, leaned out of her like gods. But it was the cars that concerned us. The immigrant cars of those soft-coal and steam days were combined day and night coaches with a cooking stove at each end. You fuelled these yourselves by picking up sticks and small bits of wood at divisional points, the compulsory change-over stop every two hundred miles. The big, rounded, wooden luggage racks pulled down into rough bunks at night. There were facing seats, for two, under each of these contraptions and we staked out a foursome right away. We could see before the train started that the filth and dirt were going to become well nigh insupportable and we meant to keep our tiny area spotless and to ourselves.

It was a marvellous journey, beginning with eight hundred miles of forest – virgin, you might say, except that all the trackside trees had long ago been burned to stumps. We decided against cookery, and lived as cheaply as we could on what we could get from a canned goods buffet car or store in the middle of the vast train. Our staple diet was beans, but our coach was always full of women rushing from the stoves with pots of horror for their men. At the far end of the train were two most strictly guarded coaches of women going through to Vancouver, a full week's journey. Iron-faced, over-bosomed matrons guarded them, and we were allowed to chat to them in daylight. They were not allowed to come to see us. I found all this very strange but women in 1925 were a long way from 'liberation'. The two end coaches of our train might very well have been an extension of Holloway Gaol. It has to be remembered that almost everyone on the train except me was travelling free, assisted by the Canadian Government, and people were not then used to the idea of 'rights' in anything that came free. If you paid nothing for what you were getting, you did what you were told. So did I of course. No one except myself knew that I had a return ticket in my bag.

As far as I know only the four of us in our enclave either shaved or washed between Quebec and Winnipeg. At every divisional point we got out and rushed about, helping wives to pick up sticks, and, in my case, never missing the change of locomotives. I also enjoyed the collections of birds – alas, all dead and stuffed – in the various 'depot houses'. In those days all that empty country was an immense bird and animal reserve. We were half a day late coming into Winnipeg, but the whole journey was over much too soon for me. I promised to write to Williams as I rushed out of the depot into the adjoining hotel to book a cheap room, write to my mother, and find the address of places offering work. They sent me to the Labour Exchange in Portage Avenue where after ten minutes' cross-examination I accepted a job as laboratory demonstration assistant in the University of Manitoba. I hurried back to the depot and found the train still there and was able to tell Williams that we had arrived in El Dorado, that I was already in a job, and that quite soon we would both be governors of provinces. As I sat in the lounge of my hotel watching men spitting tobacco juice into cuspidors, exactly as I had read about them in O. Henry's stories, it hardly occurred to me that I might one day be using my return ticket.

In the morning I went round to collect the particulars and whereabouts of my new job, only to find that I hadn't got it after all. For a job in the University, the man told me, I had to be Canadian born. He'd forgotten that. He gave me a railway ticket to a Northern Manitoba railway depot and said that I would be met there the following day by a farmer who wanted a 'hired hand'.

I was running out of money and thought a free meal might be a good idea. I took out my father's Winnipeg letter, which was to the Managing Director of the Crescent Creamery Company, Inc., and walked round to their offices. I presented my letter and was asked to wait for a minute at the end of an enormous room filled with girl typists to whom I was an object of extreme merriment. It was the plus fours of course. I had not yet learned the lesson of protective camouflage.

The Managing Director sent for coffee and buns while he

159

asked about my father, and laughed over what had brought me from Tipperary to Western Canada. He kept referring to the roughness of the country and seemed to think I had little chance of survival. After a bit he said: 'One of our customers is looking for a hired hand; I'll have a word with him.' He picked up the telephone and began, after what seemed to me in those days a lightning connection, a long conversation. He described me in some detail; he spoke of my father, 'a big man in the Old Country', he referred to me as, 'very young and strong-looking'. From time to time he said: 'Yeah; well that's real good of you', and at last he said: 'On the Headingly wagon tonight.'

He told me that Mr Innes of Kinalmeaky Farm, Headingly, Manitoba, on the prairie, five or six miles from the end of the car line and the hard roads, was looking forward to giving me work, that I was to come back with my luggage at six o'clock when a wagon collecting the Kinalmeaky milk would take me out, and that I was going to a real good employer. I said: 'What about the man I'm supposed to be going to, tomorrow?' 'Just give me the ticket and forget about him,' he said. 'If you go there he'll take one look at you and leave you standing right in the middle of Canada.' I asked him why he thought that. 'Never you mind,' he said.

I came back to the creamery yard with my bag at the right time and found a yellow truck waiting, with a gloved driver, a friendly man. Every workman I had seen since my arrival in the country wore heavy gloves; I was soon to learn about that. We drove out of town and out on to the car line to Headingly, the driver cross-questioning me all the way. After a bit there were no more houses and, at last, Headingly. That consisted of a general store, a real cracker-barrel place like an early American movie scene, with half a dozen farm houses scattered about. Before saying goodbye to me the driver delivered a short sermon. 'Don't tell any of them out there that you can do anything. Don't let on that you've ever seen a horse, or a crop of anything. Ask them to show you how to do everything they ask you to do.' He shook my hand and I got out my bag. I felt that I was in the middle of a desert; I could see in every direction for what looked liked hundreds of miles. I wasn't in a desert for long. The door of the general store – wire mosquito netting – was pushed open and a small boy shrieked: 'Come on out, all you guys, and have a look at this huge guy in short pants.' I was soon surrounded by a small group of men, all in blue overalls, who were kind to the stranger. One of them said he was called 'George' and that 'in about an hour, maybe a bit more, we'll be on our way to Kinalmeaky.' He began to tell me a story beginning: 'When we was overseas in the war . . .' I was soon to know it by heart. I still do. I heard it many many times.

My new friend, whom everyone called 'Bulling George', took me into the store to wait. The surroundings were immensely familiar, from the films. There was an apple barrel, and there were farmers standing around it in overalls talking about the price of wheat. They had strange accents but I recognised the words without any trouble. The price of wheat was too low. Has there ever been a farmer since Abel who thought that prices were too high? George had got some drinks from somewhere and was a bit tight as we got into his springless pole wagon and set off on my roughest ride until then. I have never seen a Western without remembering my first short journey on the Great Plains. Some of the 'covered wagon' people had withstood more than a year of it – and George and I were on a 'grade' track, a road thrown up from the virgin prairie by power shovels. It was dark and I had been seasick a couple of times, as I have never been when actually at sea, when we stopped at a big wooden house. 'Here we are,' said George and he dumped me and my bag on the porch and left me standing in the dark. A stout middle-aged lady opened the door and welcomed me. 'I'm Mrs Innes,' she said, a Yankee of Yankees, born and bred in Minnesota. 'Come on in and make yourself at home.' She gave me coffee and bacon, showed me into a little bedroom, told me her husband would be seeing me first thing, and that breakfast was at six. She'd bang on my door at five-thirty. 'Don't you worry,' she said. It seemed to me that she banged on my door ten minutes later.

After breakfast, Mr Innes, who had obviously been out and at work hours earlier, 'looked me over', through the black glasses he wore all the time because of cataract operations. He clearly disliked the little he could see of the tall figure in grey flannel trousers and an old cricket shirt. After a really prolonged and totally silent scrutiny he spoke. 'Another white-collared darling from the Old Country,' he said. 'I'll hang your hide on the fence before the end of the week. If you really want to work here I'll know what you're made of by dinner time.'

He took me out to the site of what was going to be a large wooden building of some kind. All round it, about three feet high, were long piles of thin planks, hairy with rusty nails. There was a loose-faced youngish man sawing at a bit of wood on a trestle. Mr Innes said: 'I've brought you a helper, Serge', and went away. 'What's your name?' said Serge. 'You know mine.' 'Kevin,' I said. 'Well listen to me, Kalvin,' said Serge, 'and I'm going to call you Kal for short. If a guy had a guy kinda sorting all that lumber into lengths and pulling out them nails a guy could get on.'

It was half past six, and I went to work. By half past twelve I knew all about working gloves as I had not much skin on either hand; I had torn my trousers and shirt, and was ready for a rest. Serge took me with him to the 'bunkhouse' in which my Gladstone bag had appeared, lying on the filthiest bed I have ever seen. Half a dozen men were sitting on similar beds. Serge introduced me: 'This is Kal; the guy can do a morning's work; he's just done one.' They all nodded at me but no one said anything. The floor was about six inches of rock-hard caked black 'gumbo', as I learned to call the soil of the prairie. It was all very dispiriting. I sat on my bed and watched scores of beetles running in and out of my mattress. In about a quarter of an hour I saw through the window a fat man come out of a hut and start banging with an iron bar on a metal disc hanging on a chain by his door. 'Grub,' said someone and we all moved across to the eating house. I was introduced to the fat man, our cook, who came from Iceland. 'Kaspar, this is Kal.' I saw at once that I wasn't going to want any dinner.

There was another long table in the room and to this came a new and quite different-looking bunch of men. Someone called out: 'Hey, you guys, we got a new one from the Old Country – Kal.' One or two of them looked round and nodded. A man beside me in khaki overalls, the only pair not blue I saw all the time I was in Canada, said, 'I'm Ed. We're teamsters, them guys over there are milkers. They bunk separate, and live separate, as we produce grade milk here. Ain't you going ter eat?' I said no but that I could eat the huge slabs of toast provided by the cook, and drink a mug of his coffee. It also occurred to me that the milk might be wonderful to drink and it was. I lived on milk and toast and pumpkin pie for six months. Our meat supply was from cows reacting to the tuberculin tests. Those cows were shot and fed to us. I didn't know that at my first meal; I just didn't like the look of it.

After this dinner we went and sat on our beds. A young man came in and spoke to me. 'I'm Paul Innes,' he said, 'the old man's son. I'm to tell you that he'll keep you a week to see how you go. You're to go out with George and the milk this evening. George'll tell you what to do.' He went away.

George was sitting on his bed in the corner. 'What we do now', he said, 'is sleep. Then at four o'clock, or maybe half past, we hitch up our horses and drive in, like I did last night, with all the milk. The guy from the creamery who brought you out from Winnipeg, or some other guy, collects it off us, I get all the truck they want from the store, and we come back same as last night, but with loads of empties, getting in here around eleven. These guys will all be asleep and we come in quiet. You're to have Darkie and Brownie.'

Ed looked up at me from his bed. 'That's the worst team on the place,' he said. 'You'd expect that, wouldn't you? Darkie bites and kicks, watch him close; Brownie's a mare and won't move much.' 'Yes, I'd expect that,' I said, and they all laughed. It seemed the moment for remembering the advice I'd been given the night before. 'I've managed horses a bit,' I said, 'but I've never harnessed one over here. Is it different? It looked different coming here last night but I couldn't see very well.' They all laughed again. 'Bulling George'll show you,' one of them said; he was Martin, the foreman, 'and if you've any dough get yourself a pair of overalls in the store and a pair of rubbers. We get a shower of rain, you won't be able to move in the gumbo in them shoes.' I had nearly five pounds left of my starvation money and I said, yes, I'd do all that. After a bit the men moved off to go on with whatever they were doing, and I sat looking at my dreadful bed. There was a massive closed stove in the bunkhouse. I pulled my mattress off the bed and piled it on top of the stove. The beetles poured out of it, hundreds of them. George was lying on his bed, filthy boots and all. 'You got the right ideas,' he said and went off to sleep.

163

There was another young man of about my own age and apparently on this milk run too, but he didn't speak, curling up and dropping straight off to sleep. I was soon to learn how to manage that. But I was rather wide awake on this first day and I went on with my sterilising operations. After a while beetles stopped coming out of my mattress, and I replaced it on the stove with two grim-looking blankets. At least nothing ran out of them. There was a none too clean sheet which I thought could be left alone. The bunkhouse began to fill with flies and I saw that our netting fly door was full of holes and rents. I started pinching and edging it together. I had no tools and didn't know where to look for any.

At four o'clock George woke up, shouted at my silent companion and then said: 'We'll get over to the barn and get started.' We walked across a space in the limitless prairie to the horse barn. It held forty Percherons, all except six out at work. They were ploughing in the sow-thistle on the summer fallow. That was where our 150 Guernsey-type cows were grazing, kept together by a man on a buckskin – a native Canadian pony. I was introduced to Darkie and Brownie and became instantly grateful to the man on the milk truck. It was pole-wagon harness, all in one piece, and I could never have managed it without a lesson or two. As it was, George first showed me how to do it, then did it for me, and I was all right with my team from then on. The horses were backed into the wagon, one each side of the pole, and hitched to it with harness straps. The pole was yoked to the horse collars by swivel hooks.

George led our little caravan of three wagons past a vast cow shed, past the milk hands' bunkhouse, and round to the bottling sheds. Here I was introduced to Carl the milk bottler, also from Iceland, who was to become a friend. All our milk was 'Grade A, Certified' which meant that it was guaranteed tubercular free, guaranteed as to fat and solids-not-fat content, and guaranteed perfect in any other way required. The milkers were examined by a doctor every single week and were fully clothed in white from head to foot; the cows were milked dry under pain of instant dismissal. Milking machines were still uncommon and unreliable. The milk reached the consumer in a bottle the contents of which had never been touched by a human hand. We filled our three wagons with crates of these bottles, the back of my wagon having in addition several churns of milk, just as good as the rest, but surplus to Grade A requirements in Winnipeg. It would be made into butter. I learned from Carl that we could drink as much milk as we wanted and I had an ice-cold bottle before we started.

It was a wonderful drive from Kinalmeaky to Headingly. There was no need to feel sick because we stood in our wagons, swaying with the 'ship'. George had brought in a seated covered wagon for me the night before, but now I was open to the sky, and I thought I could see a hundred miles in any direction. I was the last of our trio, Brownie and Darkie crawling along, not understanding my English accent and not much caring either. I heard myself singing and I don't know that I've been happier than on that first drive over the really and truly boundless prairie – just what the books had called it.

The drive back was even better. It was summer dark – not really dark at all – and the stars came out, bright, huge, almost within reach of your hand. I munched a kind of mixed toffee and chocolate bar called 'O. Henry'. I had a parcel with my overalls in it. Beside me stood my new rubbers. I was almost penniless. I could have broken a piece off the moon, but it wouldn't have turned to gold in my hand.

All went well. Every morning I worked with Serge the carpenter, a Bohunk whose parents had come to Canada from South Georgia. In the afternoons I cleaned out our bunkhouse, a most popular move, slept a little, and then did the milk run. My companions began to ask me to get messages for them from the general store, another good sign. Just before the end of my trial week I became bold enough to put forward my chief worry. I said to them all: 'I know you all sleep in your shirts and that I ought to sleep in mine as I have done so far. But I can't sleep any too well in a day shirt. Do I get shot if I wear pyjamas?' 'You're OK with us, Prince,' Ed told me, 'and you can go to bed in a blouse and skirt if that helps any.' So on the Sunday morning I put on my pyjamas and dressing gown, and all the milkers came over to pull my leg.

On my first Sunday evening Paul Innes came over and gave me ten dollars. I don't think I've ever been so glad to see actual cash money before or since. He then said: 'The Old Man says you can stay as long as you want, or until the Mounties come for you. He'll pay you forty dollars a month, all found like now, and if you're here at threshing you'll get the same bonus as the rest of the guys.' I wrote to my father pointing out that he was about to begin owing me money.

Sunday was a splendid day at Kinalmeaky. There was a strange gangly youth who on weekdays cleaned out the horse barn, taking all day over it. On Sundays, after breakfast, all the teamsters went over to the barn and did the job in an hour, having the rest of the day off. We on the milk run had to do that of course just as usual; cows don't stop work on Sundays. I shaved every afternoon in my off period, but Sunday was the great shaving day for the outfit. We heated water, just as I had sterilised my mattress, on top of the stove, and those who were going into Winnipeg to look at women, or eat at 'Murphy's Electric Lunch', put on things roughly resembling clothes. One or two of the teamsters had old Model T Fords with chains for the gumbo on all four wheels. Sometimes on a Sunday one of these would set off for the 'bright lights' packed with half our bunkhouse. Manitoba was 'dry' in those days but bottled beer could be bought. For hard liquor you had to take a room in a cheap hotel and none of us could afford that. We were an abstemious lot on the whole.

I enjoyed Sundays. I think now that I even enjoyed my third Sunday, which was the day I read the letter from my grand girl breaking everything off. She had just spent a fortnight with my parents, and I suppose that had been too much for her. I wrote and said 'All right' and spent the rest of that afternoon composing letters to other men's wives. Several of the men were illiterate and I used to write to their wives for them. The trouble had been that the men who had been writing these letters for the illiterates could not resist the chance to scribble dirt.

These wives were hundreds of miles away in the North Manitoba bush and only saw their men after 'freeze up'. In the summer, the men were away at the outfits like ours, earning money. This was the 'homesteading system' which was run by the Canadian Pacific Railway or by the State of Manitoba through the Canadian National Railway. Both had massive grants of land given on 'construction' conditions. A man tough enough to stand the life, and with the right sort of wife, could apply for a quarter section, which was 150 acres, and get it absolutely free. But he had to build a dwelling house, and break ten acres of virgin land the first year. In the second he had to begin having a bit of livestock, and also break a further acreage. If he and his wife could manage the crudity, the discomfort, the appalling loneliness of the long desperate winters, they could become proud independent farmers, making a little money, in about five or six years. And there was rich land all about them into which they could expand. But to provide stores for the winter the menfolk had to go out and work all summer long. So the wives were alone and sick for their men and the last thing they wanted was a lot of smut on dirty bits of paper.

I can remember the first letter I wrote quite clearly. It was for a Syrian who could speak English but not read or write it. I sent his wife the following:

Dear Mrs Ahmed,

You husband asks me to write to you and to say he loves you very much and misses you every day. He is well and is saving every dollar. I can assure you that he has not been off this place since I came here three weeks ago. He says that if you will write he will give me the letter to read to him and I assure you that no one else will see it. I have asked your husband to get Mrs Innes to read out this letter to him before it goes to the mail. Then he will know that you have not been distressed by the jokers in this outfit.

I signed that 'Your loving husband' and made Abdul or whatever his real name was – we called him Jake – put a cross under that. I remember how pleased I was when he refused to take the letter over to Mrs Innes. 'You ain't that kinda guy,' he said, and I still hope I ain't. It was strange that even the men who were illiterate had wives who could read and also write quite well. They used to write to their husbands for me to read out. 'Thank the guy who wrote for you. Your letter was a comfort.'

On Sunday those of us who hadn't much money or were saving it went to the ice cream parlour in St Francis Xavier. The owner had a daughter and it was delightful for us to sit and look at her. The nearest other young woman would have been in Winnipeg. It was a legend that the owner of the parlour had a shotgun under the counter and I liked to believe it was true. But I never saw a gun, only this nice smiling girl filling the wafers and cornets. Perhaps that is why I still like ice cream.

The weeks went by and the work grew harder. I was lent for a few days to a man making a bridge over a dry prairie creek – 'cricks' we called them – and my poor team had a hard time of it, and so did I, dragging at the gumbo with earth scrapers fitted with a tipping handle. One day the supervisor hit one of my horses, Darkie I expect, with the flat of a fork. I at once unhitched and walked my team back to Kinalmeaky. They all thought the boss would sack me that night but he didn't; he supported me. The supervisor came into our bunkhouse to rib me, but all the teamsters stood by me. He couldn't fight us all and we had a cheerful sing-song night instead. While I had been on loan, I had slept in a distant farm shed in an enormous bed between a negro and a deaf and dumb halfwit who could beat us both at 'horse shoe', a primitive game of quoits, thowing horse shoes at a steel peg stuck in the ground.

It became hay-cutting time. The hay was rough prairie grass in the sloughs which we called 'slews'. These great bog-like places appeared here and there on the prairie and were kept for hay because they were too wet to plough in the spring. Darkie and Brownie were just as bad and slow in a grass mower as in any other type of rig, but they were at their worst in a hay sweep. These immense pronged affairs, with the two horses many yards apart, were steered along the lines of mown dry grass and held, when fully loaded, about half a ton. This was pulled to a lift-like arrangement, also horse-worked, which, unlike a European hay and straw elevator, discharged the entire load in one cascade on to the men building the primitive ricks. The baler will have changed all that.

There were other exhausting jobs, the only limits to the hours of work being wear to machines or the possibility of overtiring horses. Men were being paid and were expendable. Looking back, I think grain crushing for cattle feed was the most totally exhausting work I have ever done, because it was a straight five-hour stretch without any possibility of rest. If you stopped for a breather the torrent of flattened oats or barley would have risen to choke the crusher. The big tractor driving it had no need to stop and no need of attention. So you went on shovelling.

We had a nasty incident that summer, filling sunflower into a tower silo. That too was a continuous process, the man inside treading out and levelling the rain of macerated sunflower leaves

168

and stalks pouring down on him and rising up in the tower with the intake. When he needed a breather – and he needed one frequently – he crept out of one of the many doors all up the side of the tower on to the enclosed ladder reaching to the summit, climbed down and stood outside on the ground for ten minutes. The important thing was to make sure that all the little doors above the silage level were open and to close each one as the silage rose up and reached it. One day we forgot. No one noticed that the levelling man inside was not appearing now and again for his 'breather' and when work stopped for the day, we brought him out a raving lunatic, shouting, weeping, and mentally collapsed. Each time he had been buried in silage he had managed to drag himself on top of it, but we could not hear his shouts for help above the roar of the cutter and blower and the tractor powering it. He was all right in a day or two but it was a nasty experience for all.

All this time I was under pressure from home. There I was, a happy teamster drawing forty dollars a month, and there was my father, quite unconscious of everything at the other end, sending almost weekly cables reading: 'Having difficulty new cultivator stop Cable method operating lifting mechanism'; or, 'Interested receive your view in extenso possibility successful breakaway move western Canada central government Quebec.' Messages of this kind delivered out from Headingly by a boy riding bareback on a buckskin to a labourer working a footlift horse-drawn hay-rake four miles from the bunkhouse were not calculated to enhance the popularity of a man who was already in strange receipt of the London *Times* weekly edition, scores of pages of parental exhortation and books from brothers and sisters.

We came to wheat cutting and wheat stooking (there were no combines yet), and at last I came into my own. For months I had been taking the wagon driver's advice and saying 'No' every time anyone asked me if I knew how to do this or that. And then one glorious day Martin, the foreman, said: 'Say, Kal, can you fix the canvases on a binder and rig up the knotter?' 'Yeah,' I said, putting everything I knew into that evocative reply. I spent all that day getting a seven-foot-six cut Massey-Harris Binder into running order and then for a wonderful fortnight I sat upon it, hitched with two similar machines, behind a great Moline tractor driven by Mr Innes's eldest son, Ray, while we flattened a couple of sections of wheat, 1,200 acres. It was a marvellous rest. Every eight sheaves you moved a foot and all eight fell to the ground in a heap from the collecting basket. Every hour or so you pulled the long string to Ray's arm and he stopped while you made some trifling adjustment. Now and again there was a stop at what in Britain would be called 'the headland' for fresh twine in the binder and knotter.

On the ground in the two sections were the supplementary labourers, paid seven dollars a day and expected to earn every cent of it. It's a long way from one end of a section to the other and these men were stooking the wheat against time, almost running. Seven dollars a day and all found was a lot of money in 1925 and took some earning. We teamsters were now drawing harvest money, seventy dollars a month, still nothing like seven dollars a day. But we were paid when it rained and the seven-dollar men were not. They slept upstairs in our bunkhouse and had their meals apart from us aristocrats. On wet days we lay on our bunks sleeping and reading while they fretted. We sang the old Canadian wet-day song: 'More rain, more rest, more hoboes in the west.' And it was with these men among us that I saw what it meant to be fired in Western Canada.

Each day a truck fitted with benches would arrive at the bunkhouse to take the men to the place of work, which on a huge outfit like Kinalmeaky could be several miles away. Just before it moved off Mr Innes, who, with his almost blind eyes, missed nothing, would come over from the house and stand looking at his strange collection of casual labour from 'the East'. Then he would point a finger: 'You're fired, and you're fired, and you're fired.' No one ever argued or pleaded for another chance. That wasn't the custom of the country. But there they were, these men, a thousand or fifteen hundred miles from home, with no money other than a bit of back pay, no job, and nowhere to go, standing alone and helpless in the middle of hundreds of thousands of square miles of prairie. When I told Mr Innes of these thoughts, he laughed at me. 'We ain't got rid of you, Kal, not yet; but a guy like you is always standing on a banana skin.'

We had two hailstorms between corn cutting and threshing, and a hailstorm on the prairie once experienced is with you for life. You hear it coming – and if you're working horses you let them out of the traces and crawl under whatever machine or wagon you're working. Hail on the prairie is an insurable risk and no wonder; lumps of ice fall out of the sky with frightful velocity and seem to be aimed straight at you. If the corn is standing it is flattened; if there is enough wind to slant the hail – and there always is – every window in the path of the storm is shattered. The noise is tremendous. The whole thing is over in five minutes. Someone has been ruined and your horses, having nowhere to go except Saskatchewan or Alberta, have come back to you. It's someone else's business to claim the insurance. You go on with your work.

There was a day when Kinalmeaky became the hottest place in the world. It was even in the European papers. We were working with horses and we were stopped because of them, not because of us. Water was sent to us every hour while we were outside and the churns in which it was brought were too hot to touch in twenty minutes, with the water in them steaming. And then suddenly there was Mr Innes, in his black glasses and, as always, in a dark jacket. 'Get in now, you guys,' he said, 'them horses can't stand a day like this.' I said that I too found it quite warm. 'I can get six of you, Kal, any day of the week,' he said, 'a good horse ain't so common.' He was a man of few words, but every one of them had a punch behind it.

It came on to threshing time. In the Canada of those days the great threshing mills were dragged about the section as each quarter was cleared. They were fitted with shredding cutters, into which the whole sheaf was pitched, and a blower which drove the subsequent chaff through a huge movable tube. As the work proceeded a great mountain of chaffed straw grew under this tube. Work began at half past four in the morning and ended when it was too dark to see. After we had put away our horses, rubbed them down, and fed them, we usually fell asleep in our boots, too tired to undress, almost too tired to move. We had our own threshing mill but the smaller men on the prairie, who had to hire travelling mills, lit the straw piles at night and worked through. This could be very dangerous. Exhausted hired men would put a rock into a sheaf and feed it in or let go of a pitching fork 'accidentally'. This stopped the work instantly of course and could cost thousands of dollars. Mr Innes reckoned that it paid him to stop the work when it was too dark for him to see what we were doing – or not doing. All the teamsters were up to all the tricks which gave them a bit of rest, the principal one being to arrive at the mill with a load of sheaves before the man in front had finished pitching off. I was slow and never once was I in that happy position. All through harvest I drew up to the mill when the man ahead of me had just finished pitching off and was driving away. All the men, except me, knew how to build a hollow load which looked like a full one. I'd learned at home how to build a harvest load and there was no point, there, in doing other than make the job such that the wagon was full and the final effect beautiful. On the prairie we were a rough lot getting through the day as best we could.

By the time harvest was over, I was drilling rye on a mile-and-a-half-long furrow behind six Percherons. Brownie and Darkie were now in the care of some new unfortunate. My father's letters and cables were becoming insistent that I should come home. I had made my point. I had not starved and I was badly needed for the Aberdeen Angus and Suffolk sheep. No one understood the operation of the Society herd and flock books, or how to enter cattle and sheep at shows, how to see them into the proper sales. Four thousand five hundred miles away from Synone, I had become an invaluable man, a lynchpin in a golden cart. I had a word with Mr Innes. 'I'll stake you to a quarter section here, Kal,' he said, 'and you'll do well in this country. But you've got a real nice soft living waiting for you back in the Old Country. You go back to it.' So I decided to go. That was one of the many, many big mistakes I have made through life.

But I still had a long way to go in Canada. We began to prepare for the freeze up, the casual labourers were all paid off and went home, as did the 'homesteaders', those strange friends for whom I wrote letters on Sundays. The teamsters who were not to be kept on for the winter began to look for jobs in Winnipeg and elsewhere as boilermen, night watchmen, caretakers, storekeepers, anything which would give them some sort of winter wage and keep them out of the cold. I was told I could stay as long as I liked – for good if I liked – but again Mr Innes thought I should go home. In the meantime we finished the building on which I had spent my first day. It proved to be a gigantic fowl house, the first completely covered fowl-run I had ever seen, and a precursor of the deep litter houses now a commonplace of the English countryside. I was now a teamster and a personage and I had no truck with fetching and carrying; I was on the roof nailing shingles, brought to me by lesser brethren. Bulling George got into a fight over that, but he was a coward at heart and gave way when his shingle carrier came at him with a hammer.

There was nothing gentlemanly about our bunkhouse. I never had to fight or defend myself, but those who did were not particular about Queensberry Rules. You used any weapon to hand and your boots as required. I think that is probably why I am never so shocked at 'hooliganism' as people think I ought to be. I've lived with roughnecks.

Real cold is something which cannot be described. Polar explorers take care not to experience it and anyhow there are places on earth colder than either pole. Mountaineers are protected in a special way for high altitude cold for a short time and not for months of daily work. Prairie cold has nothing to stop it anywhere, no trees, no hills; it is unpitying. Unlike the wet cold of Eastern Canada with its six feet of snow it is bone dry cold. A bucket of water put outside a bunkhouse will be solid to the bottom in ten minutes. It can be sixty degrees below zero on the prairie, although that is not normal. But it is not going to get warm until the spring. I had a few weeks of that, Balaclava helmets, two pairs of mitts, and then it was time for home.

Mr and Mrs Innes gave a teamsters' farewell supper for me and all the men came to it. It was our night and we made the most of it, ribbing the boss, telling him all his methods were out of date, that slavery was going out together with all his other methods. He stood it well, saying that he'd done all right, and that it didn't look as if any of us would. That he'd grown forty successive crops of wheat on the gumbo and except for the sow thistle it wasn't any different from the day he'd broken the first sod. He wasn't going to give up disc ploughs just because some son of a bitch out of college told him to, and he'd give up hand milking the very day it paid him to give it up. When that day came, he wouldn't have to lie awake worrying about how many guys he'd got on the place with clap or worse. He said he reckoned it was time for Kal to offer him a job with that father of his back in the Old Country. I said we'd be glad to have him and we all went back to the bunkhouse a little drunk.

Paul Innes took me into Winnipeg the next day, all the guys turning out to cheer me off and I felt a bit tearful. I seemed to have plenty of money and I paid a supplement on my third-class return ticket to get out of the day car on to the sleepers. I hadn't the clothes for all that grandeur, just a red and white mackinaw and overalls, but I felt I'd earned it. By the time we got to Montreal, where my ship was waiting – the *Alaunia* this time, a sister ship of the *Ascania* – I was getting a bit short. A man I made friends with on the train invited me to join him in the Windsor Hotel, but I didn't tell him I was down to fifteen dollars with three days' wait before sailing.

I found a cheap dive and paid my bill in advance. 'A guy like you don't haveta,' the clerk said. 'I do haveta,' I said. I settled for what was called American Plan. You hired the bedroom and paid cash for everything else. 'Everything else' for me was breakfast and, by the third morning, that was one roll with coffee. I spent all three days in cinemas brushing up my French from the captions, and sleeping. I got into the ship at the earliest moment allowed, twenty-four hours before cast off, and made the voyage in a four-berth cabin with only one man in it with me. He was a nice chap but he stole my mackinaw when he left the ship at Plymouth. I was penniless by then and had to stay in the ship until she was warped right up into King George V dock on the Thames. It did not occur to me that I should outlive that dock.

We were almost an empty ship. Most of the few fellow passengers I had were deportees, whores, convicts, extradition people. I found them all most agreeable. The whores, being off duty, were all prudes, the ex-convicts looking forward to being home again, the extradition men all confident of proving their innocence. They all disappeared and I was left with the problem of getting myself and my luggage to the nearest point of civilisation, my eldest brother in his tiny Clapham flat. I gave my Gladstone bag to Carter Patterson, and began to walk.

It's a long walk, rather more than twelve miles of pavement, but I had some tobacco and my pipe. I had no matches and no money to buy any, but I knew what to do; I had read it in a book, the advantage of an expensive education. I stood peering with affected deep interest into a shop window. Almost at once I was joined by people wanting to know what was absorbing this strange-looking young man in overalls. Men who pause to look in shop windows usually light up before long and at the right moment I asked one of them if I might share his match. Soon I was puffing happily along. Yes, I had tipped both my cabin and table steward, to the surprise of both. I gave them English cheques on the London Head Office of the National Bank of Ireland.

I hadn't brought anything back with me from El Dorado, but I hadn't starved on the prairie and I was home – home to the real nice soft living that was waiting for me in the old country. Alas! That was the end of the beginning.